HIDDEN LOGIC PUZZLES

by Charles Weaver

Illustrated by Sanford Hoffman

Sterling Publishing Co., Inc.   New York

To Regina ("Mom") and Gloria ("Hon").
One put me on the right path;
the other kept me there.
Both were needed . . . and still are.

10 9 8 7 6 5 4 3 2 1

Published by Sterling Publishing Company, Inc.
387 Park Avenue South, New York, N.Y. 10016
© 1992 by Charles Weaver
Distributed in Canada by Sterling Publishing
% Canadian Manda Group, P.O. Box 920, Station U
Toronto, Ontario, Canada M8Z 5P9
Distributed in Great Britain and Europe by Cassell PLC
Villiers House, 41/47 Strand, London WC2N 5JE, England
Distributed in Australia by Capricorn Link Ltd.
P.O. Box 665, Lane Cove, NSW 2066
Manufactured in the United States of America
All rights reserved

Sterling ISBN 0-8069-8334-5

CONTENTS

BEFORE YOU BEGIN

Like all others, the puzzles in this book are intended to be fun. If you learn something while solving them, so much the better.

Solving the puzzles requires nothing beyond what you learned through the 7th or 8th grade. While a knowledge of algebra might provide a more elaborate solution in some cases, it is not necessary for your success; common sense will work just as well. For some, algebra is merely disciplined common sense.

Much of what follows is really nothing more than a different perspective on ordinary things. It is a disguised attempt to break down the overly rigid thought patterns which, to one degree or another, afflict us all. It has been said that, when your only tool is a hammer, every problem begins to look like a nail. When you finish this book you should realize that we are each endowed with much more than just a hammer.

Two other common kinds of rigid thinking are called vertical and horizontal thinking. If told that a treasure were buried somewhere under a football field, how would you set out to find it? A vertical thinker would choose a spot and dig a single hole all the way to China. The horizontal thinker would dig a great number of different holes, each only a few inches deep. Obviously, though not to them, neither is likely to reach his objective. By encouraging you to break such chains on your thinking, I hope this book will be both helpful and entertaining. Once mastered, logical thinking skills are at least as useful in dealing with everyday problems as they are in solving puzzles.

When you read each puzzle you will be standing at point A. Upon solving it you will have arrived at point B. Part of the process in getting to the correct result should be to ask yourself, while still at point A, two questions: "What do I know about this situation?" and "How can I apply what I know to get to point B?" If your answers to the first question are incomplete or incorrect, the journey may be a long and difficult one. With good answers to the first question and a plan of attack to guide you, the trip will be much shorter. Horizontal, vertical or hammer thinking will only slow you down.

By looking at a puzzle (or problem) from several perspectives you may be surprised by how much you do know about it. Having only one perspective, however, often leads to gridlock. So, if you get stuck, revisit point A and start again. If all else fails, the answers are provided in the back of the book.

Traditionally, we have been taught unidirectional thinking: always start at the beginning and proceed through a strict sequence of steps, in *one* direction, toward the solution. If we are then given a starting point in the middle or at the end of a problem, this does not work. The hidden logic in many of the number puzzles and TOURnaMENT really involves being able to change from uni- to multidirectional thinking. Given, for example, the answer to a traditional long division problem, can you work both forward and backwards (depending on where you start) to get to the question? Unlike the traditional approach, you also get to choose the starting point, but the logic of long division does not change. Unfortunately, some people never learned the logic but, instead, memorized a rather mechanical, one-way procedure to solve such problems.

The hidden logic of cryptograms, etc., lies in knowing which letters appear most often in our language, what letters can follow an apostrophe, certain letter combinations (What letter will nearly always follow a "q"?) and so on. Educated guessing may also help if it is based on logic and knowledge of our language. For example, given TH _, common sense tells us that the missing letter is probably an E.

Jotto41 involves more logic than meets the eye. Starting with the process of elimination, you may be able to narrow down the possibilities. Then, by considering letter combinations and using trial and error, you can often arrive at the solution. It may look and sound easy but you may find it about as easy as trying to nail a quivering piece of gelatin to a tree using only one hand.

When you successfully complete a puzzle, give yourself a small pat on the back. If you learned something in the process, a larger pat is in order. Above all else, have fun.

TOURnaMENT

TOURnaMENT, as far as I know, is my creation. The idea for it came to me during the NCAA "sweet sixteen" playoffs. Sixteen teams (A–P) are invited to play in a tournament as shown in the middle column of the grid. In the first round of play (A vs B, C vs D, etc.), winners advance to the major league playoffs (to the right of center) and losers move to the minor league playoffs (left to center). From that point on, teams advance (to the right or left) until they lose. Can you figure out which team should replace each star in the grids that follow to end up with the complete results of the tournament? Can you then finish these grids based on nothing but logic? These puzzles may help you to get your brain in gear before you engage your pencil.

The solution is found on page 93.

The solution is found on page 95.

The solution is found on page 97.

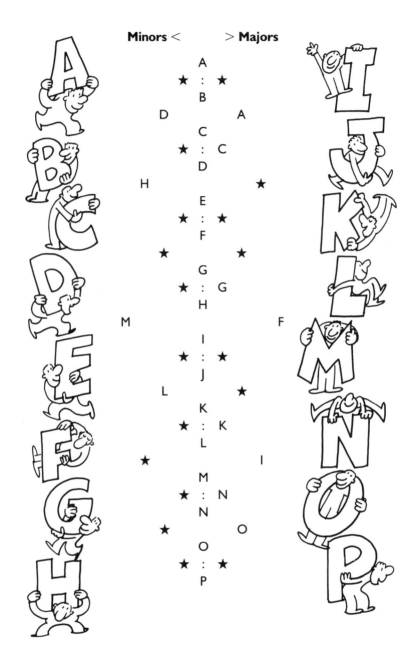

The solution is found on page 100.

Minors $<$ $>$ **Majors**

The solution is found on page 102.

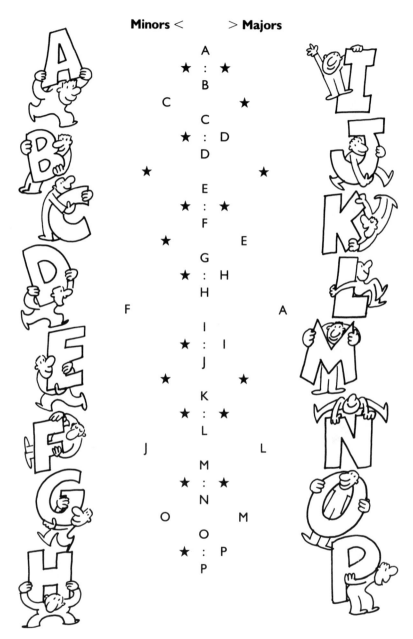

Minors < > Majors

The solution is found on page 104.

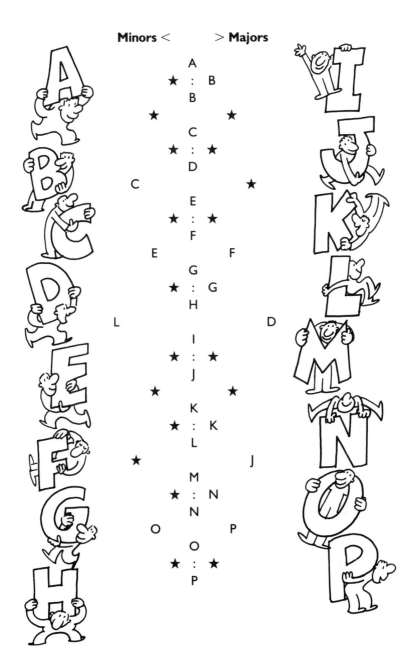

Minors <   > **Majors**

The solution is found on page 107.

The solution is found on page 109.

The solution is found on page III.

The solution is found on page 112.

The solution is found on page 115.

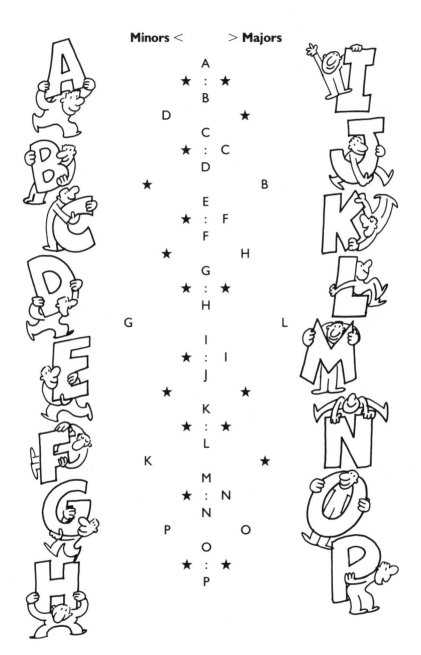

The solution is found on page 116.

Minors < > Majors

The solution is found on page 119.

Minors < > **Majors**

A
★ : ★
B
C ★
C
★ : D
D
★ ★
E
★ : F
F
★ H
G
★ : ★
H
E B
I
★ : J
J
L K
K
★ : ★
L
N M
M
★ : ★
N
★ ★
O
★ : O
P

The solution is found on page 120.

The solution is found on page 123.

NINE-BY-NINE

Here we have a puzzle which, among other things, tests your ability to follow directions. To complete this puzzle you must put a single-digit number into each empty space (shown with a •) in such a way that no digit is repeated in any row, column or any of the 3 × 3 squares. By requiring that no digit be repeated in any row, column or 3 × 3 square, we have uniquely specified the problem. All that is left is to figure out where to start and how many starting points you may need in a particular puzzle. Both are good questions and, I trust, you will come up with good answers.

The solution is found on page 95.

The solution is found on page 93.

The solution is found on page 97.

The solution is found on page 100.

The solution is found on page 102.

The solution is found on page 104.

The solution is found on page 107.

27

The solution is found on page 109.

The solution is found on page 111.

The solution is found on page 112.

The solution is found on page 115.

The solution is found on page 116.

The solution is found on page 119.

The solution is found on page 120.

The solution is found on page 123.

JOTTO41

These are based on an old game called Jotto in which players are given clues and try to guess the word held by an opponent. Jotto41 is a solitaire version ("for one"—41). Will Shortz, editor of *Games Magazine*, was the first person I know of to do such puzzles. As you will soon discover, they involve much more logic than you may think.

The number following each clue tells you how many letters in that clue also appear in the secret word, but it does not tell you which letters or in what positions they appear. By deduction and elimination, determine the five letters in the secret word and, if needed, rearrange them to get that word.

In the cases where a given clue has no letters in common with the secret word, you may wish to start by crossing out all such letters in *every* clue. It then becomes a matter of further elimination, letter combinations, and trial and error.

LOGAN—2
WAFER—0
ANGEL—2
RAPID—2
VISTA—1
IDLES—3
HALVE—1
BAKED—2

The solution is found on page 93.

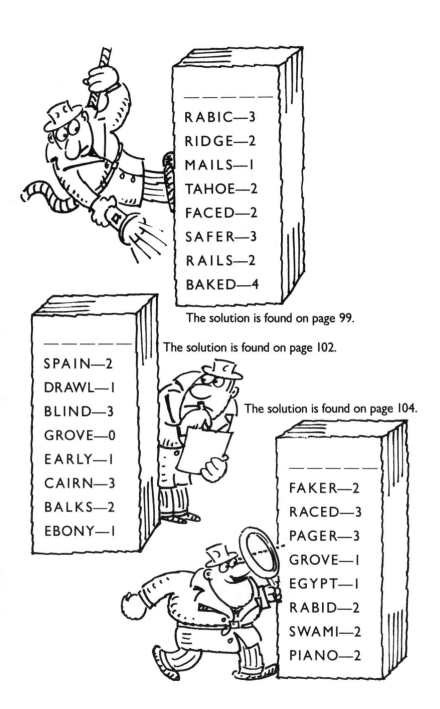

RABIC—3
RIDGE—2
MAILS—1
TAHOE—2
FACED—2
SAFER—3
RAILS—2
BAKED—4

The solution is found on page 99.

The solution is found on page 102.

SPAIN—2
DRAWL—1
BLIND—3
GROVE—0
EARLY—1
CAIRN—3
BALKS—2
EBONY—1

The solution is found on page 104.

FAKER—2
RACED—3
PAGER—3
GROVE—1
EGYPT—1
RABID—2
SWAMI—2
PIANO—2

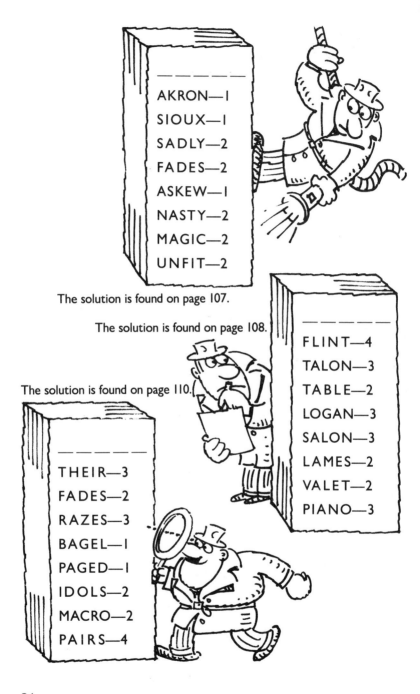

—————
AKRON—1
SIOUX—1
SADLY—2
FADES—2
ASKEW—1
NASTY—2
MAGIC—2
UNFIT—2

The solution is found on page 107.

The solution is found on page 108.

—————
FLINT—4
TALON—3
TABLE—2
LOGAN—3
SALON—3
LAMES—2
VALET—2
PIANO—3

The solution is found on page 110.

—————
THEIR—3
FADES—2
RAZES—3
BAGEL—1
PAGED—1
IDOLS—2
MACRO—2
PAIRS—4

34

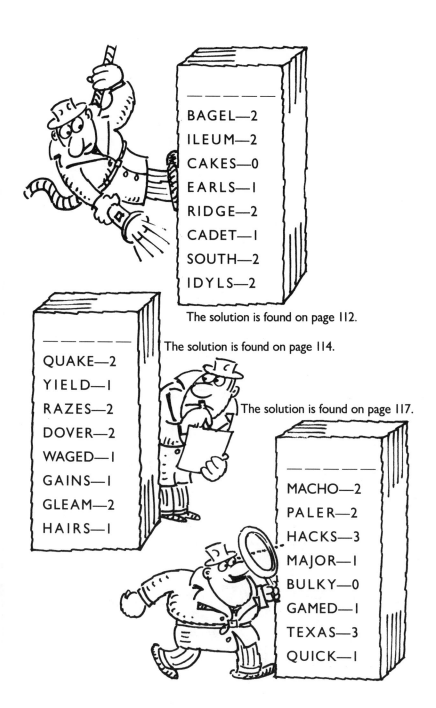

BAGEL—2
ILEUM—2
CAKES—0
EARLS—1
RIDGE—2
CADET—1
SOUTH—2
IDYLS—2

The solution is found on page 112.

The solution is found on page 114.

QUAKE—2
YIELD—1
RAZES—2
DOVER—2
WAGED—1
GAINS—1
GLEAM—2
HAIRS—1

The solution is found on page 117.

MACHO—2
PALER—2
HACKS—3
MAJOR—1
BULKY—0
GAMED—1
TEXAS—3
QUICK—1

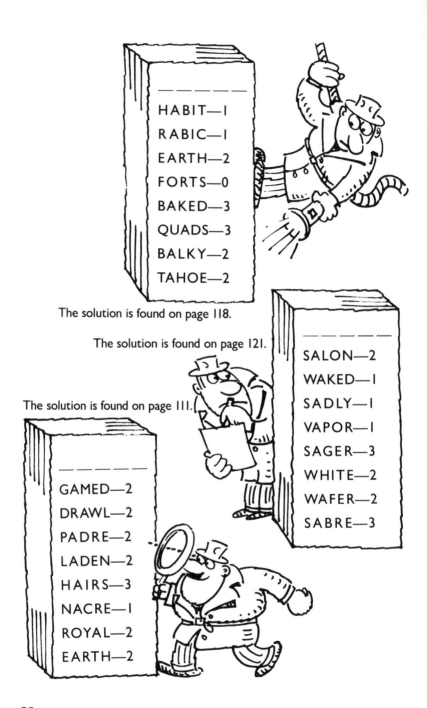

HABIT—1
RABIC—1
EARTH—2
FORTS—0
BAKED—3
QUADS—3
BALKY—2
TAHOE—2

The solution is found on page 118.

The solution is found on page 121.

SALON—2
WAKED—1
SADLY—1
VAPOR—1
SAGER—3
WHITE—2
WAFER—2
SABRE—3

The solution is found on page 111.

GAMED—2
DRAWL—2
PADRE—2
LADEN—2
HAIRS—3
NACRE—1
ROYAL—2
EARTH—2

UMIAK—3
FABLE—1
NASTY—2
NADIR—2
SHADY—2
WAFER—2
RABID—2
LIBYA—2

The solution is found on page 122.

The solution is found on page 125.

UMIAK—2
DALES—3
BURMA—2
QUALM—2
RIDGE—2
PAGED—3
BEACH—2
EARLY—2

The solution is found on page 109.

NASTY—2
SHADY—2
GREAT—3
VALET—2
KOREA—2
RACED—2
HURON—1
WAGED—3

LONG DIVISION

There are actually two kinds of long division puzzle here. The *substitution* variety consists of all letters; the *fill-in* is a mixture of letters and numbers. Either way, the object is the same: to replace the letters with single-digit numbers resulting in an arithmetically correct long division problem.

Each letter in a *fill-in* puzzle is independent of the others. Thus, several different letters may all represent the same digit within a given puzzle. In the *substitution* variety, every occurrence of the same letter will represent the same digit within a given puzzle.

Solving these problems requires you to remember what you learned about long division and, perhaps more important, what you may *not* have learned (but discovered on your own). Part of the logic involved is to find a good starting point and, if need be, to work in *both* directions from there. With the substitution puzzles, locating any 0s and 1s would be a start.

The solution is found on page 96.

```
                    1 A B 4
2 C D 0 | E F 5 G 0 H I
          2 6 J 0
            4 6 K L
            M 6 N O
            P 0 Q 0 5
            R S T U V
              1 W 7 X 7
              1 Y 7 Z 0
                  9 9 7
```

```
                          R R S T
          V V Q X | W W Q W R V Y
                    V V Q X
                    R R Y U R
                    V V Q X
                    V X Z T V
                    V Y U V W
                      X R R S Y
                      Z S Y Q Q
                      U R Y U
```

The solution is found on page 93.

The solution is found on page 98.

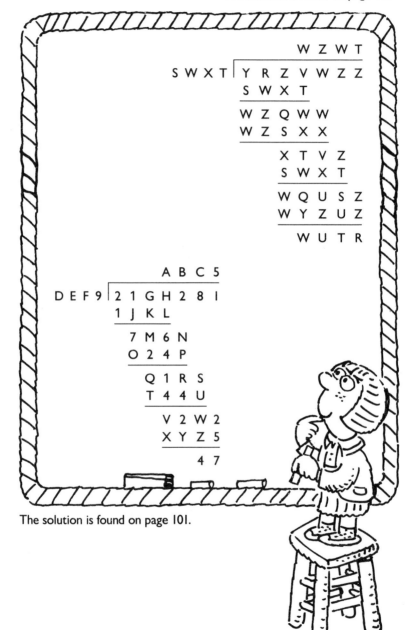

```
                              W Z W T
        S W X T  Y R Z V W Z Z
                 S W X T
                 W Z Q W W
                 W Z S X X
                     X T V Z
                     S W X T
                     W Q U S Z
                     W Y Z U Z
                       W U T R
```

```
                 A B C 5
  D E F 9  2 1 G H 2 8 1
           1 J K L
             7 M 6 N
             O 2 4 P
             Q 1 R S
             T 4 4 U
             V 2 W 2
             X Y Z 5
               4 7
```

The solution is found on page 101.

The solution is found on page 103.

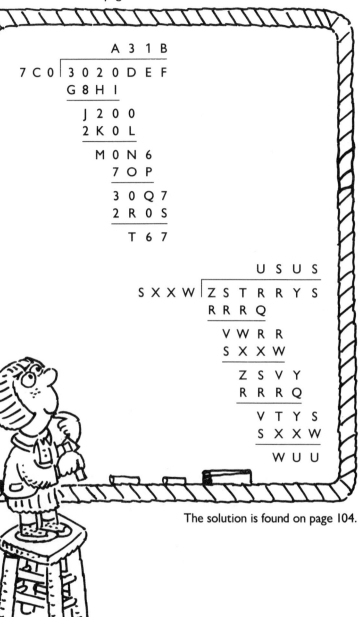

```
                A  3  1  B
  7 C 0 | 3 0 2 0 D E F
        G 8 H I
          J 2 0  0
          2 K 0 L
            M 0 N 6
              7 O P
            3 0 Q 7
            2 R 0 S
              T 6 7


                        U  S  U  S
      S X X W | Z S T  R  R  Y  S
              R R R Q
              V W R R
              S X X W
                Z S V Y
                R R R Q
                V T Y S
                S X X W
                W U U
```

The solution is found on page 104.

41

The solution is found on page 106.

```
                              A  B  3  1
              2 C D 5 | 3  1  E  F  9  G  H
                        I  J  9  K
                        L  9  2  M
                        N  O  8  P
                           7  Q  4  9
                           R  1  8  S
                              T  U  4  4
                              V  W  9  X
                              Y  4  9
```

```
                  W  Y  Q  W
          S R Q | R  U  T  T  X  R  Z
                  R  V  R  U
                  R  Y  U  X
                  R  X  V  V
                     S  R  S  R
                     R  Q  Y  R
                     R  X  Z  Z
                     R  V  R  U
                     R  T  W
```

The solution is found on page 110.

The solution is found on page 113.

```
              Y Q V V
X S T Z | X Z Z U X R T
          X S T Z
          Y V S X R
          Y W Y Z V
            Y R T Y T
            Y W Y Z V
              W Y Y S
```

```
                  A B 4 4
    5 9 5 9 | 6 8 2 1 C D E
            5 9 F G
              8 H 2 6
              I J 5 K
              2 L 6 7 1
              2 3 M 3 N
                2 O 3 P 6
                Q R 8 3 S
                4 5 2 0
```

The solution is found on page 114.

The solution is found on page 117.

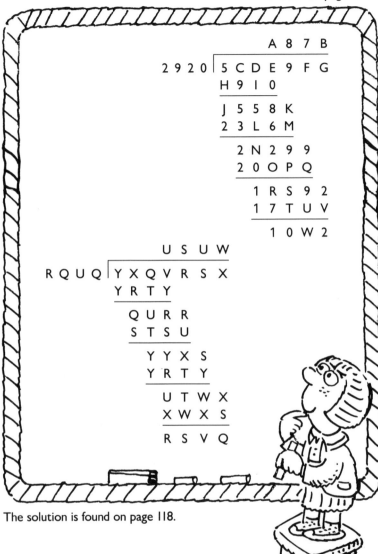

```
                    A 8 7 B
        2 9 2 0 │ 5 C D E 9 F G
                  H 9 1 0
                  ─────────
                  J 5 5 8 K
                  2 3 L 6 M
                  ─────────
                    2 N 2 9 9
                    2 0 O P Q
                    ─────────
                      1 R S 9 2
                      1 7 T U V
                      ─────────
                        1 0 W 2
```

```
                    U S U W
    R Q U Q │ Y X Q V R S X
              Y R T Y
              ───────
              Q U R R
              S T S U
              ───────
              Y Y X S
              Y R T Y
              ───────
              U T W X
              X W X S
              ───────
              R S V Q
```

The solution is found on page 118.

44

The solution is found on page 121.

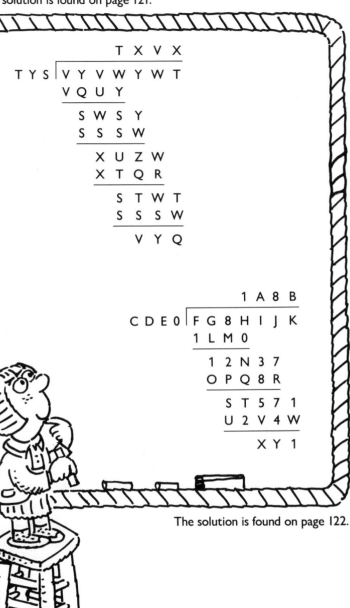

```
              T X V X
      T Y S ⟌ V Y V W Y W T
              V Q U Y
              ───────
              S W S Y
              S S S W
              ─────────
              X U Z W
              X T Q R
              ─────────
              S T W T
              S S S W
              ─────────
              V Y Q
```

```
                      1 A 8 B
      C D E 0 ⟌ F G 8 H I J K
                1 L M 0
                ─────────
                1 2 N 3 7
                O P Q 8 R
                ─────────
                S T 5 7 1
                U 2 V 4 W
                ─────────
                X Y 1
```

The solution is found on page 122.

The solution is found on page 124.

```
                    A B 7 C
        D E 3 ⟌2 F G 2 7 1 H
              2 I J 5
                3 7 K L
                M 3 N O
                  P Q 0 2
                  R 2 S T
                    3 U 5
```

```
                  R Y U W
      R V S S ⟌R Y X T V Z V
              R V S S
                Y T U V
                Y R X Q
                  U T W Z
                  U V Q Q
                    W Y U V
                    W V Y Y
                      X W S
```

The solution is found on page 126.

The solution is found on page 96.

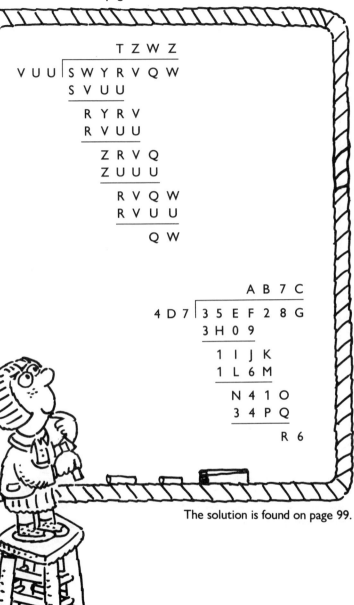

```
          T Z W Z
V U U │ S W Y R V Q W
        S V U U
          R Y R V
          R V U U
            Z R V Q
            Z U U U
              R V Q W
              R V U U
                Q W
```

```
              A B 7 C
4 D 7 │ 3 5 E F 2 8 G
        3 H 0 9
          1 I J K
          1 L 6 M
            N 4 1 O
            3 4 P Q
              R 6
```

The solution is found on page 99.

The solution is found on page 101.

```
                    5 A 7 9
        1 5 B 3 | 8 5 C D E 0 F
                  G H 1 1
                  ‾‾‾‾‾‾‾
                    J 0 0 3
                    K 7 L M
                    ‾‾‾‾‾‾‾
                    1 2 N 4 O
                    P 1 Q 8 R
                    ‾‾‾‾‾‾‾
                      1 4 S T 4
                      U 4 V 4 W
                      ‾‾‾‾‾‾‾
                        X 4 7
```

```
                  R T W U
    R R V S | S W Q T W W T
              R R V S
              ‾‾‾‾‾‾‾
              U Y Z W
              U Q Y Y
              ‾‾‾‾‾‾‾
              R W X W T
              V Z Q X
              ‾‾‾‾‾‾‾
              R W T R
```

The solution is found on page 103.

The solution is found on page 105.

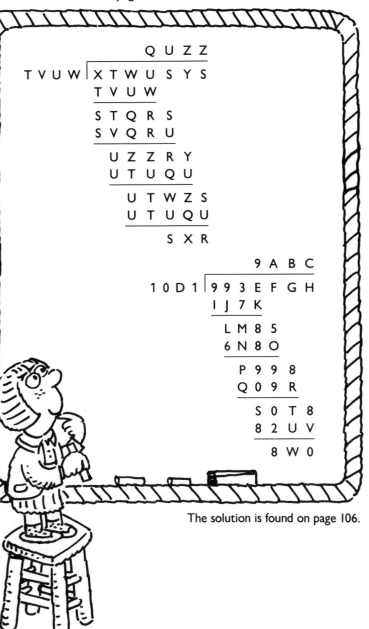

```
                    Q U Z Z
T V U W │ X T W U  S Y S
          T V U W
          S T Q  R S
          S V Q  R U
            U Z Z R Y
            U T U Q U
              U T W Z S
              U T U Q U
                  S X R
```

```
                      9 A B C
  1 0 D 1 │ 9 9 3 E F G H
            I J 7 K
            L M 8 5
            6 N 8 O
              P 9 9 8
              Q 0 9 R
                S 0 T 8
                8 2 U V
                  8 W 0
```

The solution is found on page 106.

49

The solution is found on page 110.

```
                          A B C D
        E F 7 | G 0 H 4 1 1 1
                J 7 3 K
                  L M 9 N
                  2 O 8 P
                    Q 0 3 R
                    S 4 9 T
                      5 U V 2
                      5 2 2 W
                      1 4 3
```

```
              X U R W
    Y V V | T Y T T R V Y
            T R X X
              Q Y Z R
              Q W U U
                R V Q V
                V W R R
                  Q R Z Y
                  X Y W W
                    X T R
```

The solution is found on page 113.

The solution is found on page 114.

```
              S V Q V
ZQRZ)S R T X Z W R
        S V Q S
          V T T Z
          V Z Y V
            V Y W R
            V Z Y V
              X Z V
```

```
                A 9 4 B
      C 5 6)D E F 5 7 G H
            1 1 4 8
              1 J 7 K
              L M 0 N
                7 3 9
                O P Q
                1 R S 8
                T U 9 V
                  W 6
```

The solution is found on page 117.

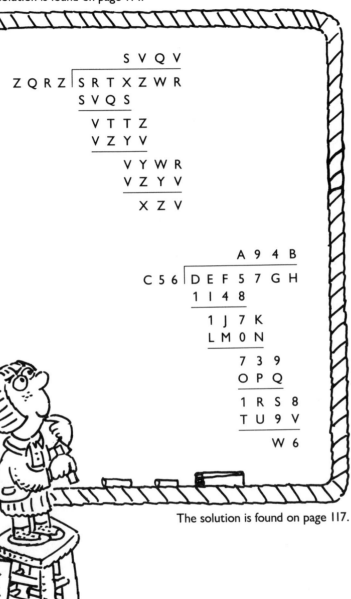

The solution is found on page 118.

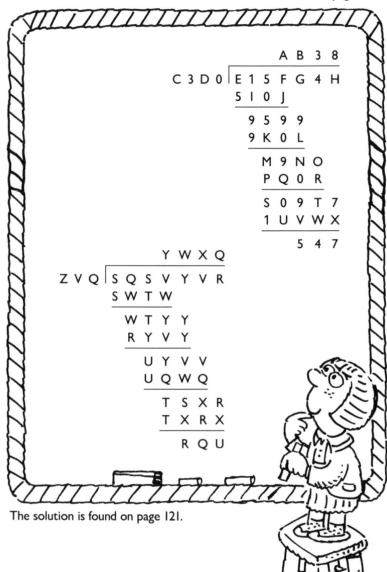

```
                        A B 3 8
            C 3 D 0 | E 1 5 F G 4 H
                      5 1 0 J
                        9 5 9 9
                        9 K 0 L
                          M 9 N O
                          P Q 0 R
                          S 0 9 T 7
                          1 U V W X
                            5 4 7
```

```
                    Y W X Q
        Z V Q | S Q S V Y V R
                S W T W
                  W T Y Y
                  R Y V Y
                    U Y V V
                    U Q W Q
                      T S X R
                      T X R X
                        R Q U
```

The solution is found on page 121.

The solution is found on page 122.

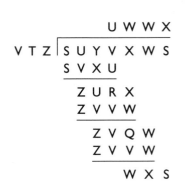

```
              U W W X
    V T Z ) S U Y V X W S
            S V X U
            Z U R X
            Z V V W
              Z V Q W
              Z V V W
                W X S
```

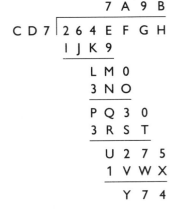

```
                  7 A 9 B
        C D 7 ) 2 6 4 E F G H
                I J K 9
                L M 0
                3 N O
                P Q 3 0
                3 R S T
                  U 2 7 5
                  1 V W X
                    Y 7 4
```

The solution is found on page 125.

DIAL-A-QUIP &
DIAL-A-THEME

Both of these puzzle types use an ordinary telephone dial or
keypad as a magic decoder ring. The number 2, for example,
is associated with the letters A, B and C on a phone dial.
Thus, any 2 which appears in one of the puzzles must be one
of those three letters. Since the dial has no letter equivalents
for the numbers 0 and 1, you will not find these digits in any
of the puzzles. Nor will you find the letters Q or Z in any of the
answers, or on a phone dial.

With only three possible replacements for any digit, these
puzzles are easier than standard cryptograms, and you may
wish to use them as warm-ups before working on the Quiptograms. Dial-A-Theme puzzles are the easiest, since each
group shares a common theme.

As far as I know, I am the originator of these puzzle vari-
eties. I started doing them after developing a curiosity about
vanity phone numbers (for instance, a jeweler whose phone
number is D-I-A-M-O-N-D).

U.S. Presidents & Vice Presidents

(1) 846627 533337766 & 22766 2877

(2) 84363673 766738358 & 2427537 9. 324722657

(3) 927736 4. 4273464 & 225846 26654343

(4) 9455426 62546539 & 427738 2. 462278

(5) 52637 6234766 & 436743 2546866

The solution is found on page 103.

U.S. States and Capitals

(1) 548853 7625, 27526727

(2) 7258 5253 2489, 8824

(3) 6596742, 9274464866

(4) 24762725, 66784 325682

(5) 743773, 76884 325682

The solution is found on page 95.

Dial-A-Quip

(1) 26 3468478 47 2 737766 946 47 63837 46 36828 288 63836 46 37767.

(2) 843 737766 946 36376'8 7323 427 548853 238268243 6837 663 946 226'8.

(3) 43 968 366'8 879, 968 226'8 3245.

(4) 663 4363728466 752687 87337; 2668437 4387 843 74233.

(5) 84373 47 6663 76 3323 27 43 946 3637 668 547836.

The solution is found on page 98.

Major League Baseball Teams PAST and Present

(1) 645928533 2739377

(2) 3387648 844377

(3) 8676686 2583 5297

(4) 78. 56847 276967

(5) 726 372624726 442687

The solution is found on page 97.

56

Dial-A-Quip

(1) 3672849, ... 9687 7246 46 69 43278.

(2) 6684464 324637 5453 26 36789 269.

(3) 27748464 15 6468837 32759 6659 4827268337 2
30-646883 9248.

(4) 746753 765884667 735366 273.

(5) 9474464 26678637 27 6824 363749 27 75266464.

The solution is found on page 102.

U.S. Presidents & Vice Presidents

(1) 23652646 42774766 & 5384 7. 667866

(2) 52637 (54669) 227837 & 925837 3. 6663253

(3) 2272426 5462656 & 42664225 426546

(4) 766253 732426 & 436743 2874

(5) 436743 9274464866 & 5646 23267

The solution is found on page 94.

The NBA Teams—PAST and Present

(1) 639 537739 6387

(2) 567 2643537 25477377

(3) 726 372624726 92774677

(4) 9274464866 2855387

(5) 64264 4328

The solution is found on page 95.

Dial-A-Quip

(1) 6684464 62537 87 238837 547836377 8426 4327464 687 6263 636846633.

(2) 2 788 47 2 47283 9484 843 3637 542533 688.

(3) 7822377 47 668 2 5687639, 288 2 33784628466.

(4) 84373 47 66 7822377 9484688 7475.

(5) 5433 47 9428 4277367 86 87 94453 93'73 625464 75267 367 5433.

The solution is found on page 124.

58

Dial-A-Quip

(1) 968 366'8 37696 29 3255464 4686 843 92837, 288 29 7829464 46 48.

(2) 339 844647 273 2732833 263 737332833 28 843 7263 666368.

(3) 9687 5433 47 668 2 37377 734327725.

(4) 7822377 26637 46 2267; 3245873 46 226'87.

(5) 43 946 46385437, . . . 285437.

The solution is found on page 126.

U.S. States and Capitals

(1) 46665858, 429244

(2) 5225766, 64774774774

(3) 9274464866, 34787428 63 26586242

(4) 252269, 639 9675

(5) 267866, 6277224873887

The solution is found on page 97.

The NFL Teams—PAST and Present

(1) 726 34346 24274377

(2) 639 9675 442687

(3) 463426276547 26587

(4) 2833256 24557

(5) 47336 229 7225377

The solution is found on page 104.

Dial-A-Quip

(1) 3267 366'8 266 66263437.

(2) 93 226668 2668765 843 9463. 93 226 235878 687 72457.

(3) 843 6678 76543 78663 46 2 787828873 47 843 569378 46 843 3686328466.

(4) 9428 93 733 3373637 624659 66 9428 93 5665 367.

(5) 246423, 668 242623, 3383764637 3378469.

The solution is found on page 99.

Dial-A-Quip

(1) 567377 259297 4283 26 392873. 9466377 259297
4283 26 4332.

(2) 26-673728466 47 2576 267732859 7735533 9484 896
5388377—93.

(3) 843 2378 929 86 3378769 26 36369 47 86 6253 446
9687 374363.

(4) 9436 7663663 3362637 25463 623343623, 968'3 23 2
3665 668 86 7335.

(5) 9436 255 84465 25453, 66 663 844657 8379 6824.

The solution is found on page 100.

U.S. States and Capitals

(1) 6234766, 947266746

(2) 7768433623, 74633 475263

(3) 65524662 2489, 65524662

(4) 867352, 526727

(5) 7253444, 66784 22765462

The solution is found on page 107.

The NHL Teams—PAST and Present

(1) 744523357442 359377

(2) 78. 56847 25837

(3) 567 2643537 54647

(4) 7488728744 73648467

(5) 2254279 352637

The solution is found on page 109.

Dial-A-Quip

(1) 338228466'7 7877673 47 86 7375223 26 36789 6463 9484 26 6736 663.

(2) 843 566953343 8428 2 732738 394787 47 4253 63 843 732738.

(3) 46257 273 373267 9484 332354637.

(4) 2424678 38379 47328 & 66253 36332867 78263 2 6455466 63346273 64637.

(5) 843 33937 843 32287, 843 78766437 843 6746466.

The solution is found on page 105.

Dial-A-Quip

(1) 366'8 3837 2663873 4273 9675 9484 4273 84465464.

(2) 242623 328677 6659 84673 946 5669 469 86 26878 437.

(3) 366844 47 228632623 86 843 9473.

(4) 7243623 47 63837 637359 566953343; 48 47 6733759 566953343.

(5) 75327873 46 843 562 7887 7373328466 46 843 9675.

The solution is found on page 106.

U.S. Presidents & Vice Presidents

(1) 52637 6234766 & 35274343 43779

(2) 52637 5. 7655 & 436743 6. 325527

(3) 9455426 4. 8238 & 52637 7. 7437626

(4) 596366 2. 5646766 & 482378 4. 48674739

(5) 2272426 5462656 & 263739 5646766

The solution is found on page 101.

The NFL Teams—PAST and Present

(1) 2442246 23277

(2) 325527 2692697

(3) 639 3645263 72874687

(4) 7328853 73242957

(5) 7463649 227346257

The solution is found on page 116.

Dial-A-Quip

(1) 843 6659 844647 93 5337 273 843 844647 93 4483 2929.

(2) 6659 843 932737 56697 94373 843 7463 7462437.

(3) 2 666539 46 7455 47 78455 2 666539.

(4) 84373'7 2 47328 3433373623 2389336 5669464 2 84464 & 8633778263464 48.

(5) 33277 273 33822833 4686 87 263 226, 43 93 9474, 23 33822833 688.

The solution is found on page 125.

64

Dial-A-Quip

(1) 4363767489 44837 2774782623, 728437 8426 238423.

(2) 4663789 7297, 288 48 36376'8 729 366844 367 7663 736753.

(3) 843 745837 546464 47 327437 86 3463 46 7663663 3573'7 25683.

(4) 63837 4483 238423 46 2 27693.

(5) 3245873 47 26 38368, 63837 2 737766.

The solution is found on page 115.

U.S. Presidents & Vice Presidents

(1) 9455426 43679 42774766 & 5646 89537

(2) 9663769 945766 & 846627 7. 62774255

(3) 394448 3. 3473646937 & 7424273 6. 64966

(4) 263739 5225766 & 5646 2. 2254686

(5) 846627 533337766 & 436743 2546866

The solution is found on page 112.

The NBA Teams—PAST and Present

(1) 645928533 28257

(2) 465336 78283 92774677

(3) 3678 92963 7478667

(4) 567 2643537 525377

(5) 4687866 7625387

The solution is found on page 105.

Dial-A-Quip

(1) 2 746453 3228 9455 63836 77645 26 46837378464 27486368.

(2) 48 47 238837 86 5669 6684464 8426 86 53276 6684464.

(3) 43 946 427 2 246423 427 8768253.

(4) 738853 663 3433428589 263 968 5337 48637337 2929.

(5) 4663 422487 273 27 3279 86 3676 27 223 6637.

The solution is found on page 111.

Dial-A-Quip

(1) 843 6659 929 86 4283 2 374363 47 86 23 663.

(2) 6253 843 6678 63 96877353, 367 8428 47 255 84373 47 63 968.

(3) 9463837 92687 86 73224 2 3478268 4625 6878 8253 6269 76255 78377.

(4) 2 73724 46 843 768 47 238837 8426 2 725666 46 843 732.

(5) 87884 427 66 7732425 8463 63 487 696. 487 4687 47 669—259297.

The solution is found on page 123.

U.S. Presidents & Vice Presidents

(1) 37265546 743723 & 9455426 7. 5464

(2) 7424273 6. 64966 & 437253 7. 3673

(3) 8597737 7. 47268 & 43679 945766

(4) 52637 6234766 & 326435 8. 86675467

(5) 7424273 6. 64966 & 77476 8. 24639

The solution is found on page 119.

U.S. States and Capitals

(1) 287846, 83927

(2) 26586287, 6446

(3) 77746434353, 45546647

(4) 435362, 6668262

(5) 463426276547, 4634262

The solution is found on page 109.

Dial-A-Quip

(1) 43 946 226668 32623 252637 843 35667.

(2) 328587 273 84425 94373 5683 47 8446.

(3) 238368873 47 5878 2 76626842 9673 367 8768253.

(4) 84373 47 66 7824 84464 27 32756377, 6659 2 3245873 86 733.

(5) 87328 9687 48378 27 2 48378 367 896 3297; 8436 4483 446 2 463.

The solution is found on page 120.

Dial-A-Quip

(1) 86 83224 47 86 53276 89423.

(2) 66 663 63337 2 732473 367 53386837 5627837.

(3) 4 773337 843 373267 63 843 388873 86 843 4478679 63 843 7278.

(4) 27483 367 9687 54648284667 263, 7873 366844, 8439'73 96877.

(5) 366'8 2868. 246 688 63 843 2255 7275.

The solution is found on page 124.

Major League Baseball Teams— PAST and Present

(1) 267866 272837

(2) 2852682 272837

(3) 225846673 6746537

(4) 639 9675 9265337

(5) 2442246 94483 769

The solution is found on page 107.

69

The NHL Teams—PAST and Present

(1) 639 537739 338457

(2) 639 9675 7264377

(3) 42783673 9425377

(4) 267866 278467

(5) 94664734 5387

The solution is found on page 116.

Dial-A-Quip

(1) 64637 273 5453 7272248837; 8439 6659 38628466 9436 6736.

(2) 77228423 3637 668 6253 7373328; 7373328 77228423 62537 7373328.

(3) 949 668 46 688 66 2 5462? 8428'7 94373 843 37848 47.

(4) 269663 946'7 259297 7247464 843 7663 727359 427 6824 46 843 28842.

(5) 6684464 2437 736753 5453 668 84465464.

The solution is found on page 125.

QUIPTOGRAMS

These are standard cryptogram puzzles. By looking for apostrophes, letter frequencies and certain letter combinations, you should be able to get started. (In our language, the most to least frequently occurring letters are: E, T, A, O, I, N, S, H, R, D, L, U, C, M, P, F, Y, W, G, B, V, K, J, X, Z, and Q.) Then it becomes a matter of finding the letters which will complete a word. Each group of five quiptograms shares the same substitution pattern.

(1) T dprjsh ztei fpss mzihr dymps tr prihkhdiprj tkjvbhri.

(2) Pz qmv otxh t jtklhr trl t spuktkq, qmv otxh tss qmv rhhl.

(3) Rm mrh rhhld t khepyh zmk shzimxhk smudihk.

(4) lohkh pd rm dveehdd fpiomvi kpdn.

(5) Pz qmvk dopy lmpy lmhdr'i embh pr, dfpb mvi im pi.

The solution is found on page 94.

(1) Xuolwag jm kuy yng wemgkxg ub bgwl, eoy yng dwmygl ub jy.

(2) Buui dg ukxg, mnwdg uk tuo; buui dg yrjxg, mnwdg uk dg.

(3) W zglxn jk yng zuy jm egyygl ynwk w mwiduk jk yng mgw.

(4) W xljyjx jm w zglmuk rnu fkurm yng rwt eoy xwk'y vljqg yng xwl.

(5) Agkjom nwm ijdjywyjukm. Myozjvjyt jm euokvigmm.

The solution is found on page 96.

(1) Cjhhqj vaj flssldtqi naf ivt mjje utafojfc nzni.

(2) Huj pvcc dna fv naihulax ls uj ethc cvbjvaj jqcj'c blaf hv lh.

(3) Vaqi huj zjnojo mavzc zujoj huj cuvj eladujc.

(4) Hndh lc huj noh vs dvawladlax ejveqj hunh huji mavz bvoj huna ivt fv.

(5) Ls ivt fva'h hoi, ivt dna'h snlq.

The solution is found on page 98.

(1) Gbwtejpa ujp zbp twhwai nplluipl dp lpae zq zwnpl dp dwtt aphpj lpp.

(2) Lwnrtp lqtmzwqal lpteqn ujp.

(3) Bp dbq aphpj nuep u nwlzusp, aphpj nuep u ewlgqhpjc.

(4) Zbp ewkkpjpagp fpzdppa qjewaujc uae pyzjuqjewaujc wl u twzztp PYZJU.

(5) Iqqe bufwzl ujp ul pulc zq kqjn ul fue qapl.

The solution is found on page 108.

(1) Cdeoiy djh pojyi zkeahey, ichq zcdoqy.

(2) Vkw djh acdi vkw djh achq qkekfv oy gkkboql.

(3) Achq dgg icoqb dgobh, qk kqh icoqby nhjv rwzc.

(4) D rkqbhv oq yogb oy yiogg d rkqbhv.

(5) Zcogfjhq cdnh rkjh qhhf kp rkfhgy icdq zjoiozy.

The solution is found on page 110.

(1) Kiyynkk tk lvu b wvizlno, miu b snkutlbutvl.

(2) Qtgn tk cdbu dbeenlk uv ik cdtqn cn'zn jbrtlp eqblk gvz qtgn.

(3) Cdnl udn dvzkn tk snbs, pnu vgg.

(4) Tplvzblyn svnkl'u rtqq ovi, miu tu jbrnk ovi kcnbu b qvu.

(5) Ovi'zn ntudnz pznnl bls pzvctlp vz zten bls zvuutlp.

The solution is found on page 113.

(1) Ri bpoohv bhovkhs vxi rgou. Ri bpo puztev htk epgse.

(2) Nht pki nhtod pv pon pdi ga nht pki lspoogod ahk vhchkkhr.

(3) Uho'v agou aptsv; agou p kiciun.

(4) Vxiki pki vxkii godkiugiove go sgai: sipkogod, ipkogod pou nipkogod.

(5) P bpousi sheie ohvxgod wn sgdxvgod pohvxik bpousi.

The solution is found on page 99.

(1) Qbg fdei nbt jcbo d kdg zisqvkbc dzg jcbo d kiqszzic bz avi jsggmi.

(2) Dcqti jbc nbtc msosadasbzf dzg, ftci izbtqv, avin'ci nbtcf.

(3) Zieic qsei dgesxi sz d xċbhg.

(4) Odui avi obfa bj nbtcfimj, jbc avda sf dmm avici sf bj nbt.

(5) Fsmiza qcdasatgi sfz'a eicn otxv tfi ab dznbzi.

The solution is found on page 118.

(1) Gmo qolg nfe gt jolgwte fi oioke pl gt kfyo mpk etzw uwpoij.

(2) Fsfpilg oaowe swofg & itqro oijofatw lgfij f kprrpti kojptbwo kpijl.

(3) Etz jti'g jwtni qe ufrrpis pigt gmo nfgow, qzg qe lgfepis pi pg.

(4) Gwofg etzw szolg fl f szolg utw gnt jfel; gmoi spao mpk f mto.

(5) Gmo tire nfe gt mfao f uwpoij pl gt qo tio.

The solution is found on page 126.

75

(1) Jvqgwnornu on jusqosv urvrljujvq.

(2) Vsqgovl rljn hjshcj comj vsq qgovmovl.

(3) Qgj urv ags urmjn vs uonqrmjn ysjn vsq wnwrcct urmj
rvtqgovl.

(4) Xdoqoxonu xsujn jrnojd qgrv xdrkqnurvngoh.

(5) Oq on fjqqjd qs mvsa vsqgovl qgrv qs cjrdv vsqgovl.

The solution is found on page 99.

(1) Acj kfd efbq fdalehds acj ifdl njl dcl qbqualehds acj ifdl.

(2) Octhljmq ho f sccm wtfkq lc bhohl njl f wccu wtfkq lc
olfa.

(3) Vhdmo fuq thpq wfufkejlqo; leqa cdta zjdklhcd ieqd
cwqd.

(4) Lefl iehke ho nuhqz, hz hl nq sccm, ho sccm lihkq cbqu.

(5) Ehdmohsel ho fd qrfkl okhqdkq.

The solution is found on page 121.

(1) Rttxdjhz yat twtanmftat. Pt htjsxt.

(2) Ft mfg fyz y ufgdut fyz saglpxt.

(3) Salsf fyz jg zotudyx sdct gr dsz gmj. Dsz fgla dz jgm—yxmynz.

(4) Tjglhf dz ypljeyjut sg sft mdzt.

(5) Ngl uyj ols lo y myxx ga pldxe y padeht; sft ufgdut dz nglaz.

The solution is found on page 122.

(1) Dah zpmthq mpjpjy pz hrzphq dx gpjn pj zxkhxjh hmzh's emxfn.

(2) Dah zapi pj dah arqoxq pz zrgh, ofd dard'z jxd sard pd srz krnh gxq.

(3) P iqhghq dah nqhrkz xg dah gfdfqh dx dah apzdxqv xg dah irzd.

(4) Yhddpjy hthj daqxsz hthqvdapjy xfd xg ormrjeh.

(5) Rjv gxxm erj eqpdpepuh, exjnhkj rjn exkimrpj—rjn kxzd nx.

The solution is found on page 124.

(1) Hls yuvh vuzwc vhups wp k vhebqhbes wv hls zursvh wp hls mubpckhwup.

(2) Hls hewqn wv aeurwpa bo rwhlubh aeurwpa uzc.

(3) Hls osevup rlu cusvp'h eskc lkv zwhhzs kcjkphkas ujse ups rlu qkp'h.

(4) Rlsp tub pssc vkzh, vbake rup'h cu.

(5) Kp sauhwvh wv k osevup rlu wv psjse wp cubgh gbh umhsp wp seeue.

The solution is found on page 126.

(1) Qhlo sbiieua shy upgzyv ig tbiiuk, atbee upgzyv ig rhp.

(2) Bcdupizku ha fzai b kgtbpihl rgkc wgk ikgzseu.

(3) Yhdu ngzkauew qukthaahgp ig wbhe.

(4) Hw ivu ykbaa ha ykuupuk gp ivu givuk ahcu, wukihehxu ngzka.

(5) Wkuucgt ha pgivhpy tgku ivbp b lvbplu ig cg suiiuk.

The solution is found on page 98.

MAGIC SQUARES & STARS

These curiosities have been around for centuries. Mathematicians and other famous/infamous personae (including Benjamin Franklin and some royalty) have been fascinated with their so-called "magical properties" and have studied them extensively. Among their interesting properties is that each row, column, and diagonal has the same "magic" total.

If we borrow a concept called "degrees of freedom" from statistics (pardon my language), we may conclude that only a certain portion of the numbers in a magic square are actually free to change value. Once their values are known, the other numbers take on specific, predetermined values. The number of degrees of freedom can be found by subtracting 1 from the number of rows or columns in the square and squaring the result. A 3×3 magic square, for example, has four degrees of freedom ($3 - 1 = 2; 2 \times 2 = 4$). Therefore, if you know any four values in the square, you should be able to find the rest. If you have fewer starting values, life gets much more complicated.

Magic Stars are an interesting variation on Magic Squares. Each line-of-four has the same "magic" total, which is found in the center of the star. Given any six starting values that do not include a complete line-of-four, you should have no trouble. With fewer starting values, or with six that *do* include a complete line-of-four, what may appear to be simple can become quite challenging.

While only 10 numbers are needed to complete each puzzle, they may not be 10 consecutive (counting sequence) numbers. It is also possible to build these puzzles so that a single puzzle could have an infinite number of correct solutions. Try the easier ones and a few Magic Squares as basic training.

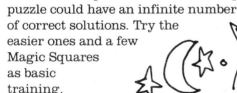

The solution is found on page 105.

140	176	212		60		132
172	208	48	56	92		136
204	44		88	124	160	168
40	76		120		164	200
72	80	116	152	188		
				192	32	
108	144	180		28	64	100

840 ▲ MAGIC TOTAL ▼ 238

39	48	57	10	19	28	
	56		18	27		
	15	17		35	44	46
14	23	25	34	43	45	54
22		33		51	53	13
30			50	52	12	21
31		49	58	11		29

The solution is found on page 96.

The solution is found on page 101.

276	28	32		260	44	48	
56		236	68	72	224		
	208	204	100	104		188	116
180	124	128	168	164	140		152
148	156		136				120
184	112	108	196		96	92	212
216	80		228	232	64	60	
52	252	256	40	36		272	24

1200 ▲ MAGIC TOTAL ▼ 141

22	13	38			
37	27		30		10
8	35	19	14		24
23	6		28		
36	26		31	20	11
15		18	9	40	25

The solution is found on page 106.

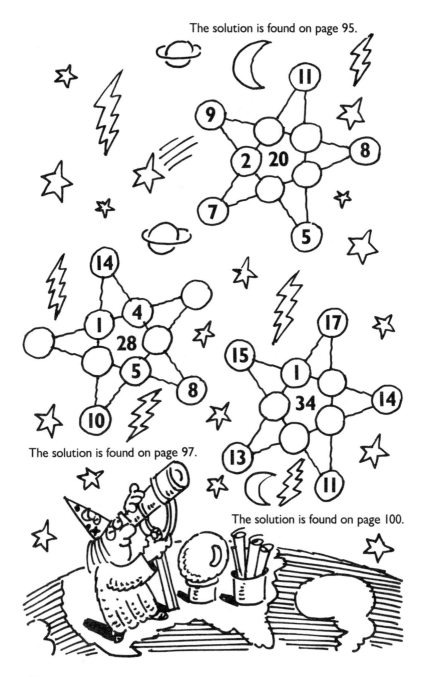

The solution is found on page 95.

11
9
2 20
8
7
5

14
1 4
28
5
8
10

The solution is found on page 97.

17
15
1
34
14
13
11

The solution is found on page 100.

82

The solution is found on page 103.

392	480	568	656	24	112	200	288	
472	560	648		104	192	280		384
552	640	80	96	184		360	448	
632	72	160					456	544
64			256		432	520	536	
144		248	336	424			616	56
224	240	328		504	592	608	48	136
304	320	408	496	584	600	40	128	216
312	400	488	576		32	120	208	296

3096 ▲ MAGIC TOTAL ▼ 342

153			126
54			
90	72		117
45			18

The solution is found on page 121.

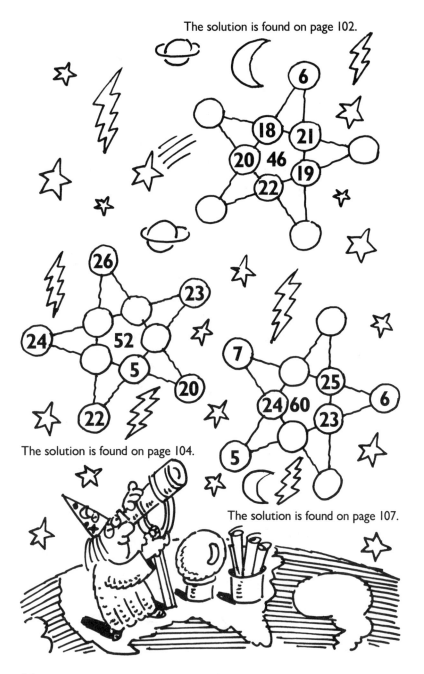

The solution is found on page 102.

The solution is found on page 104.

The solution is found on page 107.

The solution is found on page 108.

284	224	348	56	120		184	388	92	160
416		128	300		372	72	168	260	236
100	308	256	360	84		268	216	400	44
232		60	156	292		408	20	116	336
	172	280	204	384	28		320	244	344
	180	396		112	328	220	356	96	152
412	40	124							188
104	316	252	352	88	140	276			48
	364	64	148	296	240	404	24	108	332
76	176	272	248	380	36	132	312	208	340

2180 ▲ MAGIC TOTAL ▼ 324

135		117
99		81

The solution is found on page 113.

85

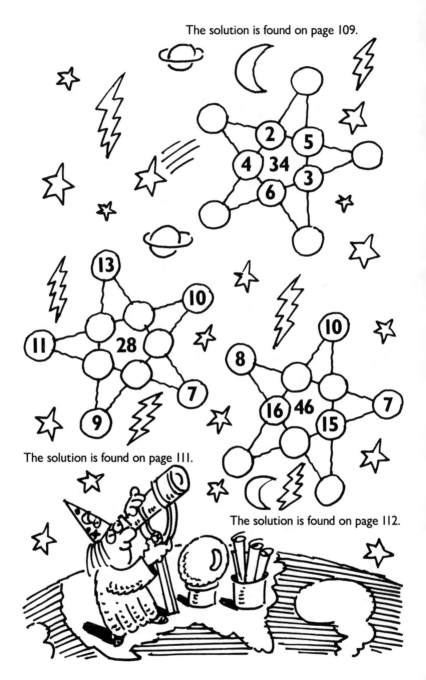

The solution is found on page 109.

The solution is found on page 111.

The solution is found on page 112.

The solution is found on page 110.

44					64
	54		60	42	20
	70		28	82	
46	12		56		78
72		34	62	40	22
30	68	36	18	80	50

282 ▲ MAGIC TOTAL ▼ 324

72	10	11	69	68	14		65
17	63	62		21	59		24
			28			50	32
	34	35	45	44	38	39	41
40	42	43	37		46		33
49		30	52	53	27	26	56
57	23		60	61	19	18	64
	66	67	13	12	70		9

The solution is found on page 113.

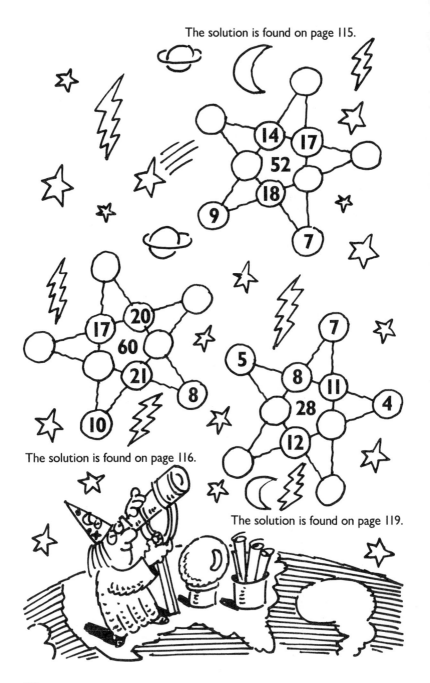

The solution is found on page 115.

The solution is found on page 116.

The solution is found on page 119.

The solution is found on page 122.

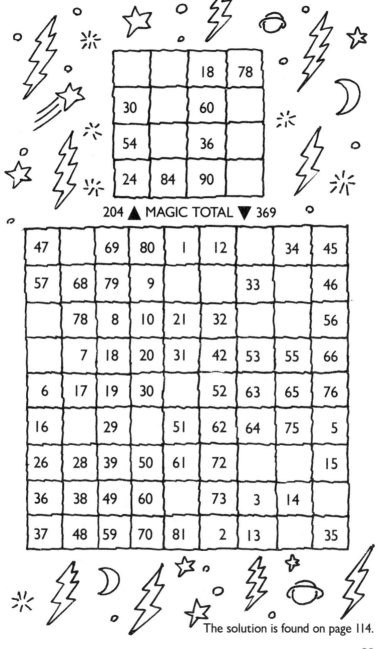

		18	78
30		60	
54		36	
24	84	90	

204 ▲ MAGIC TOTAL ▼ 369

47		69	80	1	12		34	45
57	68	79	9			33		46
	78	8	10	21	32			56
	7	18	20	31	42	53	55	66
6	17	19	30		52	63	65	76
16		29		51	62	64	75	5
26	28	39	50	61	72			15
36	38	49	60		73	3	14	
37	48	59	70	81	2	13		35

The solution is found on page 114.

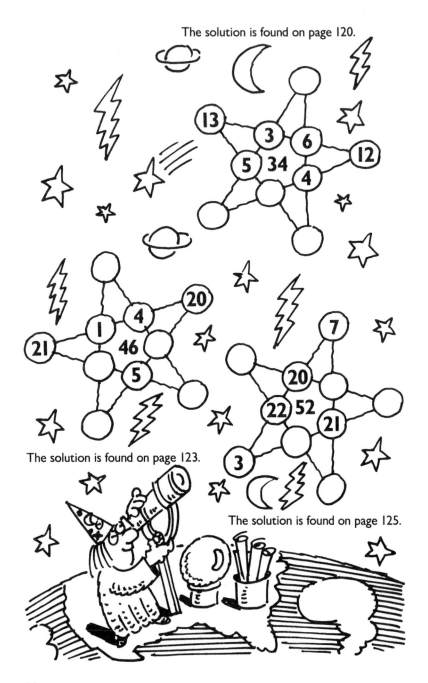

The solution is found on page 120.

13

3

6

5 34

4

12

20

4

1

46

21

5

7

20

22 52

21

3

The solution is found on page 123.

The solution is found on page 125.

The solution is found on page 124.

63	98	49

210 ▲ MAGIC TOTAL ▼ 585

75		91	18		85	50	101		44
		36	79	53	97	22	46	69	63
29		68			40	71		104	15
62			43	77	52	106	9		
21	47	74	55	100	11	38		65	90
76	49	103	17	32	86	59	93	28	42
107	14		80		98	24	45	70	51
30		67	92	26	39	73	57		16
54	95	20	41	78	64		10	31	87
23	48	72		99	13	37	82	56	89

The solution is found on page 117.

The solution is found on page 94.

144		196	222	248	10	36	62		114	140
168	194	220		30			86	112	138	142
192	218		28	32	58	84	110	136	162	166
216		26		56	82	108	134	160	164	190
240	24	50	54	80	106	132	158	184	188	214
22	48	74	78		130	156	182	186	212	238
46	72			128	154	180	206	210	236	20
70	96	100	126	152	178		208	234		44
94	98	124	150	176		228	232	16	42	68
118			174	200	226	230	14	40	66	
	146	172		224	250	12	38		90	

1430 ▲ MAGIC TOTAL ▼ 510

126	168	30	72	
	54			120
48	60	102	144	
84				
90	132	174	36	78

The solution is found on page 118.

SOLUTIONS

Solution for page 9.

```
            A
        B : A
            B
    B           C
            C
        D : C
            D
  B                 C
            E
        F : E
            F
    F               H
            G
        G : H
            H
N                       M
            I
        I : J
            J
    I               L
            K
        K : L
            L
  N                     M
            M
        N : M
            N
    N               M
            O
        P : O
            P
```

Solution for page 39 (bottom).

```
                    1 1 9 7
5 5 8 4 | 6 6 8 6 1 5 0
          5 5 8 4
          1 1 0 2 1
            5 5 8 4
            5 4 3 7 5
            5 0 2 5 6
              4 1 1 9 0
              3 9 0 8 8
                2 1 0 2
```

Solution for page 25 (top).

2	1	6	5	4	9	7	8	3
9	8	3	7	6	1	5	4	2
4	5	7	8	3	2	6	9	1
6	9	5	3	1	7	4	2	8
3	2	4	6	5	8	9	1	7
1	7	8	2	9	4	3	6	5
5	3	1	9	2	6	8	7	4
7	6	2	4	8	5	1	3	9
8	4	9	1	7	3	2	5	6

Solution for page 32. The secret word is: BLIND

Solution for page 71.

(1) A single fact will often spoil an interesting argument.
(2) If you have a garden and a library, you have all you need.
(3) No one needs a recipe for leftover lobster.
(4) There is no success without risk.
(5) If your ship doesn't come in, swim out to it.

Solution for page 92 (top).

144	170	196	222	248	10	36	62	88	114	140
168	194	220	246	30	34	60	86	112	138	142
192	218	244	28	32	58	84	110	136	162	166
216	242	26	52	56	82	108	134	160	164	190
240	24	50	54	80	106	132	158	184	188	214
22	48	74	78	104	130	156	182	186	212	238
46	72	76	102	128	154	180	206	210	236	20
70	96	100	126	152	178	204	208	234	18	44
94	98	124	150	176	202	228	232	16	42	68
118	122	148	174	200	226	230	14	40	66	92
120	146	172	198	224	250	12	38	64	90	116

Solution for page 57 (bottom).

(1) Benjamin Harrison & Levi P. Morton
(2) James (Jimmy) Carter & Walter F. Mondale
(3) Abraham Lincoln & Hannibal Hamlin
(4) Ronald Reagan & George Bush
(5) George Washington & John Adams

Solution for page 10.

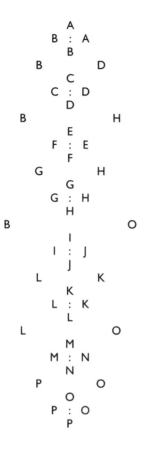

Solution for page 82 (top).

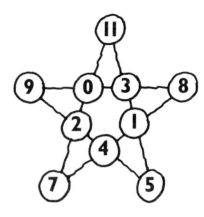

Solution for page 24.

7 4 9	6 3 2	5 1 8
2 1 8	5 9 4	6 3 7
3 6 5	1 8 7	9 2 4
9 2 6	8 4 5	3 7 1
8 7 3	9 6 1	2 4 5
4 5 1	7 2 3	8 9 6
6 8 4	2 7 9	1 5 3
5 9 7	3 1 6	4 8 2
1 3 2	4 5 8	7 6 9

Solution for page 55 (bottom).

(1) Little Rock, Arkansas
(2) Salt Lake City, Utah
(3) Olympia, Washington
(4) Bismarck, North Dakota
(5) Pierre, South Dakota

Solution for page 58 (top).

(1) New Jersey Nets
(2) Los Angeles Clippers
(3) SAN FRANCISCO WARRIORS
(4) Washington Bullets
(5) Miami Heat

Solution for page 39 (top).

```
                    1 1 7 4
2 6 9 0 | 3 1 5 9 0 5 7
          2 6 9 0
          -------
          4 6 9 0
          2 6 9 0
          -------
          2 0 0 0 5
          1 8 8 3 0
          -----------
              1 1 7 5 7
              1 0 7 6 0
              ---------
                  9 9 7
```

Solution for page 47 (top).

```
                  9 3 6 3
5 0 0 | 4 6 8 1 5 2 6
        4 5 0 0
        -------
        1 8 1 5
        1 5 0 0
        -------
            3 1 5 2
            3 0 0 0
            -------
              1 5 2 6
              1 5 0 0
              -------
                  2 6
```

Solution for page 72 (top).

(1) Courage is not the absence of fear, but the master of it.

(2) Fool me once, shame on you; fool me twice, shame on me.

(3) A perch in the pot is better than a salmon in the sea.

(4) A critic is a person who knows the way but can't drive the car.

(5) Genius has limitations. Stupidity is boundless.

Solution for page 80 (bottom).

39	48	57	10	19	28	37
47	56	16	18	27	36	38
55	15	17	26	35	44	46
14	23	25	34	43	45	54
22	24	33	42	51	53	13
30	32	41	50	52	12	21
31	40	49	58	11	20	29

Solution for page 56 (bottom).

(1) Milwaukee Brewers
(2) Detroit Tigers
(3) Toronto Blue Jays
(4) ST. LOUIS BROWNS
(5) San Francisco Giants

Solution for page 59 (bottom).

(1) Honolulu, Hawaii
(2) Jackson, Mississippi
(3) Washington, District of Columbia
(4) Albany, New York
(5) Boston, Massachusetts

Solution for page 25 (bottom).

2 7 9	3 5 8	6 4 1
8 4 1	6 9 7	3 5 2
5 3 6	4 1 2	9 8 7
9 8 3	1 7 6	5 2 4
1 2 5	9 3 4	8 7 6
7 6 4	2 8 5	1 9 3
3 1 7	8 2 9	4 6 5
6 9 2	5 4 3	7 1 8
4 5 8	7 6 1	2 3 9

Solution for page 11.

Solution for page 82 (middle).

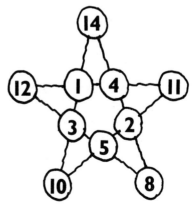

Solution for page 40 (top).

```
                1  9  1  7
2  1  3  7 │ 4  0  9  8  1  9  9
            2  1  3  7
            1  9  6  1  1
            1  9  2  3  3
                  3  7  8  9
                  2  1  3  7
                  1  6  5  2  9
                  1  4  9  5  9
                     1  5  7  0
```

Solution for page 72 (bottom).

(1) Settle one difficulty and you keep hundreds away.

(2) The boss can do anything if he puts someone else's mind to it.

(3) Only the wearer knows where the shoe pinches.

(4) Tact is the art of convincing people that they know more than you do.

(5) If you don't try, you can't fail.

Solution for page 78 (bottom).

(1) Pick battles big enough to matter, small enough to win.

(2) Adventure is just a romantic word for trouble.

(3) Give yourself permission to fail.

(4) If the grass is greener on the other side, fertilize yours.

(5) Freedom is nothing more than a chance to do better.

Solution for page 56 (top).

(1) An egotist is a person who is never in doubt but often in error.

(2) The person who doesn't read has little advantage over one who can't.

(3) If you don't try, you can't fail.

(4) One generation plants trees; another gets the shade.

(5) There is none so deaf as he who does not listen.

Solution for page 47 (bottom).

```
              7 3 7 0
4 8 7 | 3 5 8 9 2 8 6
        3 4 0 9
          1 8 0 2
          1 4 6 1
              3 4 1 8
              3 4 0 9
                  9 6
```

Solution for page 33 (top). The secret word is: BRAKE

Solution for page 74 (bottom).

(1) We cannot control the wind. We can adjust our sails.

(2) You are young at any age if you are planning for tomorrow.

(3) Don't find fault; find a remedy.

(4) There are three ingredients in life: learning, earning and yearning.

(5) A candle loses nothing by lighting another candle.

Solution for page 76 (top).

(1) Enthusiasm is emotion management.

(2) Nothing ages people like not thinking.

(3) The man who makes no mistakes does not usually make anything.

(4) Criticism comes easier than craftsmanship.

(5) It is better to know nothing than to learn nothing.

Solution for page 60 (bottom).

(1) Fans don't boo nobodies.

(2) We cannot control the wind. We can adjust our sails.

(3) The most solid stone in a structure is the lowest in the foundation.

(4) What we see depends mainly on what we look for.

(5) Choice, not chance, determines destiny.

Solution for page 61 (top).

(1) Losers always have an excuse. Winners always have an idea.

(2) Co-operation is also correctly spelled with two letters—WE.

(3) The best way to destroy an enemy is to make him your friend.

(4) When someone demands blind obedience, you'd be a fool not to peek.

(5) When all think alike, no one thinks very much.

Solution for page 12.

```
                A
          B  :  A
             B
      D            A
             C
          D  :  C
             D
  H                    F
             E
      E  :  F
             F
  H                F
             G
      H  :  G
             H
M                    F
             I
      J  :  I
             J
  L                I
             K
      L  :  K
             L
  M                I
             M
      M  :  N
             N
  M                O
             O
      P  :  O
             P
```

Solution for page 26 (top).

8 5 3	6 4 1	2 7 9
1 7 9	2 3 5	6 4 8
4 6 2	7 9 8	3 1 5
3 1 6	9 5 2	4 8 7
9 8 4	3 6 7	1 5 2
5 2 7	8 1 4	9 3 6
6 9 5	1 8 3	7 2 4
2 3 8	4 7 6	5 9 1
7 4 1	5 2 9	8 6 3

Solution for page 82 (bottom).

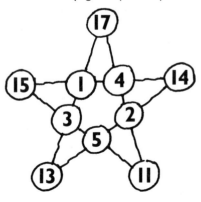

100

Solution for page 48 (top).

```
                    5 3 7 9
1 5 8 3 | 8 5 1 5 3 0 4
          7 9 1 5
          ───────
            6 0 0 3
            4 7 4 9
            ───────
            1 2 5 4 0
            1 1 0 8 1
            ─────────
              1 4 5 9 4
              1 4 2 4 7
              ─────────
                  3 4 7
```

Solution for page 40 (bottom).

```
                      1 5 1 5
1 4 4 9 | 2 1 9 5 2 8 2
          1 4 4 9
          ───────
            7 4 6 2
            7 2 4 5
            ───────
              2 1 7 8
              1 4 4 9
              ───────
                7 2 9 2
                7 2 4 5
                ───────
                    4 7
```

Solution for page 63 (bottom).

(1) James Madison & Elbridge Gerry
(2) James K. Polk & George M. Dallas
(3) William H. Taft & James S. Sherman
(4) Lyndon B. Johnson & Hubert H. Humphrey
(5) Abraham Lincoln & Andrew Johnson

Solution for page 81 (top).

276	28	32	264	260	44	48	248
56	240	236	68	72	224	220	84
88	208	204	100	104	192	188	116
180	124	128	168	164	140	144	152
148	156	160	136	132	172	176	120
184	112	108	196	200	96	92	212
216	80	76	228	232	64	60	244
52	252	256	40	36	268	272	24

Solution for page 57 (top).

(1) Empathy, . . . your pain in my heart.

(2) Nothing echoes like an empty box.

(3) Arriving 15 minutes early only guarantees a 30-minute wait.

(4) Simple solutions seldom are.

(5) Wishing consumes as much energy as planning.

Solution for page 33 (middle). The secret word is: CLINK

Solution for page 13.

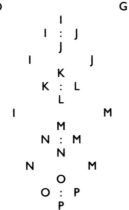

```
            A
      B  :  A
            B
   D           C
            C
      D  :  C
            D
D                  G
            E
      F  :  E
            F
   H           G
            G
      H  :  G
            H
D                  G
            I
      I  :  J
            J
   I           J
            K
      K  :  L
            L
 I                 M
            M
      N  :  M
            N
   N           M
            O
      O  :  P
            P
```

Solution for page 26 (bottom).

3	2	9	8	5	6	4	1	7
6	1	7	4	9	2	8	5	3
5	8	4	1	7	3	9	6	2
9	6	8	7	2	4	5	3	1
7	3	5	9	8	1	6	2	4
2	4	1	3	6	5	7	9	8
8	7	2	6	3	9	1	4	5
4	9	3	5	1	8	2	7	6
1	5	6	2	4	7	3	8	9

Solution for page 84 (top).

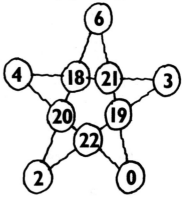

Solution for page 48 (bottom).

```
                1 7 0 8
1 1 9 2 | 2 0 3 7 0 0 7
          1 1 9 2
            8 4 5 0
            8 3 4 4
              1 0 6 0 7
                9 5 3 6
                1 0 7 1
```

Solution for page 41 (top).

```
              4 3 1 4
7 0 0 | 3 0 2 0 0 6 7
        2 8 0 0
          2 2 0 0
          2 1 0 0
            1 0 0 6
              7 0 0
              3 0 6 7
              2 8 0 0
                2 6 7
```

Solution for page 55 (top).

(1) Thomas Jefferson & Aaron Burr

(2) Theodore Roosevelt & Charles W. Fairbanks

(3) Warren G. Harding & Calvin Coolidge

(4) William McKinley & Garret A. Hobart

(5) James Madison & George Clinton

Solution for page 83 (top).

392	480	568	656	24	112	200	288	376
472	560	648	88	104	192	280	368	384
552	640	80	96	184	272	360	448	464
632	72	160	176	264	352	440	456	544
64	152	168	256	344	432	520	536	624
144	232	248	336	424	512	528	616	56
224	240	328	416	504	592	608	48	136
304	320	408	496	584	600	40	128	216
312	400	488	576	664	32	120	208	296

Solution for page 41 (bottom).

```
                5   1   5   1
1 7 7 6 | 9   1   4   8   8   3   1
          8   8   8   0
          ─────────────
              2   6   8   8
              1   7   7   6
              ─────────────
                  9   1   2   3
                  8   8   8   0
                  ─────────────
                      2   4   3   1
                      1   7   7   6
                      ─────────────
                          6   5   5
```

Solution for page 33 (bottom).

The secret word is: CRAMP

Solution for page 60 (top).

(1) San Diego Chargers
(2) New York Giants
(3) Indianapolis Colts
(4) Buffalo Bills
(5) Green Bay Packers

Solution for page 14.

```
            A
      B  :  A
         B
   C        A
         C
      C  :  D
         D
  F           A
         E
      F  :  E
         F
   F           E
         G
      G  :  H
         H
F              A
         I
      J  :  I
         J
   J           L
         K
      K  :  L
         L
   J           L
         M
      N  :  M
         N
   O           M
         O
      O  :  P
         P
```

Solution for page 27 (top).

5	4	6	1	8	2	7	3	9
2	3	9	7	6	4	1	8	5
8	1	7	3	9	5	6	2	4
6	2	1	9	4	7	8	5	3
9	5	8	6	1	3	2	4	7
4	7	3	5	2	8	9	6	1
1	9	4	2	5	6	3	7	8
7	6	5	8	3	1	4	9	2
3	8	2	4	7	9	5	1	6

Solution for page 84 (middle).

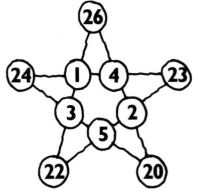

Solution for page 62 (bottom).

(1) Education's purpose is to replace an empty mind with an open one.

(2) The knowledge that a secret exists is half of the secret.

(3) Goals are dreams with deadlines.

(4) Against every great & noble endeavor stand a million mediocre minds.

(5) The fewer the facts, the stronger the opinion.

Solution for page 49 (top).

Solution for page 66 (top).

(1) Milwaukee Bucks
(2) Golden State Warriors
(3) FORT WAYNE PISTONS
(4) Los Angeles Lakers
(5) Houston Rockets

```
                              1 4 9 9
        5 0 4 6 | 7 5 6 4 2 3 2
                  5 0 4 6
                  2 5 1 8 2
                  2 0 1 8 4
                      4 9 9 8 3
                      4 5 4 1 4
                          4 5 6 9 2
                          4 5 4 1 4
                              2 7 8
```

Solution for page 80 (top).

140	176	212	24	60	96	132
172	208	48	56	92	128	136
204	44	52	88	124	160	168
40	76	84	120	156	164	200
72	80	116	152	188	196	36
104	112	148	184	192	32	68
108	144	180	216	28	64	100

Solution for page 63 (top).

(1) Don't ever confuse hard work with hard thinking.

(2) Chance favors only those who know how to court her.

(3) Enough is abundance to the wise.

(4) Science is never merely knowledge; it is orderly knowledge.

(5) Pleasure in the job puts perfection in the work.

Solution for page 42 (top).

```
                1  3  3  1
2 3 9 5 | 3 1 8 7 9 9 4
          2 3 9 5
            7  9  2  9
            7  1  8  5
               7  4  4  9
               7  1  8  5
                  2  6  4  4
                  2  3  9  5
                     2  4  9
```

Solution for page 49 (bottom).

```
                9  6  3  8
1 0 3 1 | 9 9 3 7 5 8 8
          9 2 7 9
            6  5  8  5
            6  1  8  6
               3  9  9  8
               3  0  9  3
                  9  0  5  8
                  8  2  4  8
                     8  1  0
```

Solution for page 81 (bottom).

22	13	38	29	7	32
37	27	16	30	21	10
8	35	19	14	41	24
23	6	33	28	12	39
36	26	17	31	20	11
15	34	18	9	40	25

Solution for page 34 (top).

The secret word is: DATUM

Solution for page 61 (bottom).

(1) Madison, Wisconsin

(2) Providence, Rhode Island

(3) Oklahoma City, Oklahoma

(4) Topeka, Kansas

(5) Raleigh, North Carolina

Solution for page 69 (bottom).

(1) BOSTON BRAVES

(2) Atlanta Braves

(3) Baltimore Orioles

(4) New York Yankees

(5) Chicago White Sox

Solution for page 15.

```
            A
        A : B
            B
    C               D
            C
        C : D
            D
    C               D
            E
        E : F
            F
    E               F
            G
        H : G
            H
L                       D
            I
        I : J
            J
    L               J
            K
        L : K
            L
    L               J
            M
        M : N
            N
        O       P
            O
        O : P
            P
```

Solution for page 27 (bottom).

1	2	8	9	6	4	5	7	3
4	7	3	5	8	2	9	6	1
6	9	5	7	3	1	8	4	2
8	4	9	3	2	5	6	1	7
3	1	6	8	9	7	4	2	5
2	5	7	1	4	6	3	8	9
9	3	2	4	1	8	7	5	6
5	8	1	6	7	9	2	3	4
7	6	4	2	5	3	1	9	8

Solution for page 84 (bottom).

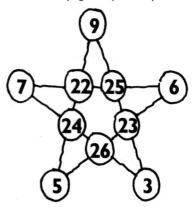

Solution for page 34 (middle).

The secret word is: FINAL

Solution for page 73 (top).

(1) Children are the living messages we send to times we will never see.

(2) Simple solutions seldom are.

(3) He who never made a mistake, never made a discovery.

(4) The difference between ordinary and extraordinary is a little EXTRA.

(5) Good habits are as easy to form as bad ones.

Solution for page 85 (top).

284	224	348	56	120	324	184	388	92	160
416	32	128	300	196	372	72	168	260	236
100	308	256	360	84	144	268	216	400	44
232	368	60	156	292	192	408	20	116	336
68	172	280	204	384	28	136	320	244	344
288	180	396	52	112	328	220	356	96	152
412	40	124	304	228	376	80	164	264	188
104	316	252	352	88	140	276	212	392	48
200	364	64	148	296	240	404	24	108	332
76	176	272	248	380	36	132	312	208	340

Solution for page 37 (bottom).

The secret word is: USAGE

Solution for page 62 (top).

(1) Philadelphia Flyers

(2) St. Louis Blues

(3) Los Angeles Kings

(4) Pittsburgh Penguins

(5) Calgary Flames

Solution for page 68 (top).

(1) Austin, Texas

(2) Columbus, Ohio

(3) Springfield, Illinois

(4) Helena, Montana

(5) Indianapolis, Indiana

Solution for page 16.

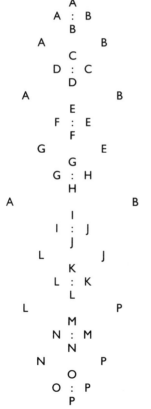

Solution for page 28 (top).

2	1	4	7	5	6	8	3	9
6	3	9	8	4	1	7	5	2
5	7	8	3	9	2	4	6	1
4	6	7	9	1	8	5	2	3
9	2	5	4	7	3	6	1	8
1	8	3	2	6	5	9	4	7
7	9	1	6	2	4	3	8	5
8	4	2	5	3	7	1	9	6
3	5	6	1	8	9	2	7	4

Solution for page 86 (top).

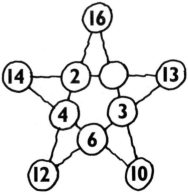

Solution for page 34 (bottom).

The secret word is: HAIRS

Solution for page 73 (bottom).

(1) Habits are first cobwebs, then chains.

(2) You are what you are when nobody is looking.

(3) When all think alike, no one thinks very much.

(4) A monkey in silk is still a monkey.

(5) Children have more need of models than critics.

Solution for page 42 (bottom).

```
              6 7 9 6
2 1 9 | 1 4 8 8 5 1 0
        1 3 1 4
        ─────
          1 7 4 5
          1 5 3 3
          ─────
            2 1 2 1
            1 9 7 1
            ─────
              1 5 0 0
              1 3 1 4
              ─────
                1 8 6
```

Solution for page 50 (top).

```
              5 4 2 7
7 4 7 | 4 0 5 4 1 1 2
        3 7 3 5
        ─────
          3 1 9 1
          2 9 8 8
          ─────
            2 0 3 1
            1 4 9 4
            ─────
              5 3 7 2
              5 2 2 9
              ─────
                1 4 3
```

Solution for page 87 (top).

44	26	76	58	14	64
74	54	32	60	42	20
16	70	38	28	82	48
46	12	66	56	24	78
72	52	34	62	40	22
30	68	36	18	80	50

Solution for page 36 (bottom).

The secret word is: SHADY

Solution for page 66 (bottom).

(1) A single fact will often spoil an interesting argument.

(2) It is better to know nothing than to learn nothing.

(3) He who has a choice has trouble.

(4) Settle one difficulty and you keep hundreds away.

(5) Good habits are as easy to form as bad ones.

Solution for page 17.

```
            A
       B  :  A
          B
    B           A
          C
       D  :  C
          D
 F                A
          E
       F  :  E
          F
    F           H
          G
       G  :  H
          H
 F                   L
          I
       J  :  I
          J
    J           L
          K
       K  :  L
          L
 P                L
          M
       N  :  M
          N
    P           M
          O
       P  :  O
          P
```

Solution for page 28 (bottom).

1 6 5	8 4 7	2 3 9
7 3 9	2 5 6	8 4 1
4 8 2	3 9 1	5 7 6
5 7 8	9 6 2	4 1 3
9 1 4	5 8 3	7 6 2
6 2 3	1 7 4	9 5 8
8 9 6	7 1 5	3 2 4
2 5 1	4 3 8	6 9 7
3 4 7	6 2 9	1 8 5

Solution for page 86 (middle).

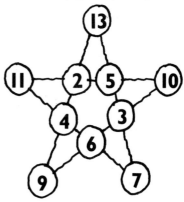

Solution for page 35 (top).

The secret word is: LIGHT

Solution for page 65 (bottom).

(1) William Henry Harrison & John Tyler

(2) Woodrow Wilson & Thomas R. Marshall

(3) Dwight D. Eisenhower & Richard M. Nixon

(4) Andrew Jackson & John C. Calhoun

(5) Thomas Jefferson & George Clinton

Solution for page 29 (top).

Solution for page 18.

5	6	1	9	8	7	2	4	3
7	4	3	2	1	6	9	8	5
8	9	2	4	3	5	1	7	6
1	7	9	3	6	2	8	5	4
3	5	8	1	9	4	7	6	2
6	2	4	5	7	8	3	1	9
9	3	6	7	5	1	4	2	8
2	1	5	8	4	9	6	3	7
4	8	7	6	2	3	5	9	1

Solution for page 86 (bottom).

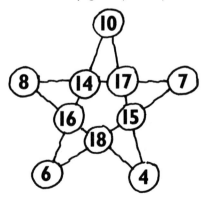

Solution for page 74 (top).

(1) Success is not a journey, but a destination.

(2) Life is what happens to us while we're making plans for life.

(3) When the horse is dead, get off.

(4) Ignorance doesn't kill you, but it makes you sweat a lot.

(5) You're either green and growing or ripe and rotting.

Solution for page 43 (top).

```
              1 0 5 5
2 8 3 9 | 2 9 9 7 2 6 3
          2 8 3 9
            1 5 8 2 6
            1 4 1 9 5
              1 6 3 1 3
              1 4 1 9 5
                2 1 1 8
```

Solution for page 50 (bottom).

```
              4 7 2 6
8 1 1 | 3 8 3 3 2 1 8
        3 2 4 4
          5 8 9 2
          5 6 7 7
            2 1 5 1
            1 6 2 2
              5 2 9 8
              4 8 6 6
                4 3 2
```

Solution for page 87 (bottom).

72	10	11	69	68	14	15	65
17	63	62	20	21	59	58	24
25	55	54	28	29	51	50	32
48	34	35	45	44	38	39	41
40	42	43	37	36	46	47	33
49	31	30	52	53	27	26	56
57	23	22	60	61	19	18	64
16	66	67	13	12	70	71	9

Solution for page 35 (middle).

The secret word is: MOUSE

Solution for page 43 (bottom).

```
              1 1 4 4
5 9 5 9 | 6 8 2 1 6 1 6
          5 9 5 9
            8 6 2 6
            5 9 5 9
            2 6 6 7 1
            2 3 8 3 6
              2 8 3 5 6
              2 3 8 3 6
                4 5 2 0
```

Solution for page 51 (top).

```
                    5 3 0 3
    1 0 6 1 | 5 6 2 7 1 9 6
              5 3 0 5
                3 2 2 1
                3 1 8 3
                  3 8 9 6
                  3 1 8 3
                    7 1 3
```

Solution for page 89 (bottom).

47	58	69	80	1	12	23	34	45
57	68	79	9	11	22	33	44	46
67	78	8	10	21	32	43	54	56
77	7	18	20	31	42	53	55	66
6	17	19	30	41	52	63	65	76
16	27	29	40	51	62	64	75	5
26	28	39	50	61	72	74	4	15
36	38	49	60	71	73	3	14	25
37	48	59	70	81	2	13	24	35

Solution for page 65 (top).

(1) Generosity gives assistance, rather than advice.
(2) Honesty pays, but it doesn't pay enough for some people.
(3) The silver lining is easier to find in someone else's cloud.
(4) Never give advice in a crowd.
(5) Failure is an event, never a person.

Solution for page 29 (bottom).

8 5 9	7 3 4	2 6 1
4 6 1	2 9 5	7 3 8
3 7 2	6 1 8	9 4 5
9 4 7	1 5 2	3 8 6
1 8 3	9 7 6	4 5 2
5 2 6	8 4 3	1 9 7
7 1 5	4 8 9	6 2 3
2 9 8	3 6 7	5 1 4
6 3 4	5 2 1	8 7 9

Solution for page 19.

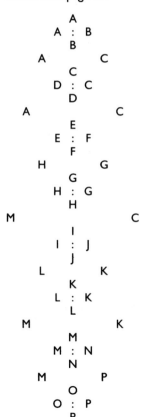

Solution for page 88 (top).

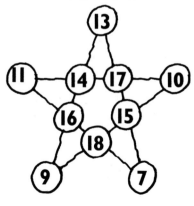

Solution for page 64 (top).

(1) Chicago Bears
(2) Dallas Cowboys
(3) New England Patriots
(4) Seattle Seahawks
(5) Phoenix Cardinals

Solution for page 70 (top).

(1) New Jersey Devils
(2) New York Rangers
(3) Hartford Whalers
(4) Boston Bruins
(5) WINNIPEG JETS

Solution for page 30 (top).

7	3	6	1	2	9	4	5	8
9	5	8	4	6	3	1	2	7
2	1	4	5	8	7	6	9	3
6	9	1	8	3	4	2	7	5
8	7	2	6	1	5	9	3	4
3	4	5	7	9	2	8	6	1
1	8	3	9	7	6	5	4	2
4	6	7	2	5	1	3	8	9
5	2	9	3	4	8	7	1	6

Solution for page 20.

```
            A
      A  :  B
         B
   D           B
         C
      D  :  C
         D
G                  B
         E
      E  :  F
         F
   G           H
         G
      G  :  H
         H
G                      L
         I
      J  :  I
         J
   K           L
         K
      K  :  L
         L
   K           L
         M
      M  :  N
         N
   P           O
         O
      P  :  O
         P
```

Solution for page 88 (middle).

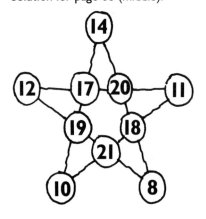

116

Solution for page 35 (bottom).

The secret word is: PACTS

Solution for page 44 (top).

```
                1 8 7 6
2 9 2 0 | 5 4 7 8 9 9 2
          2 9 2 0
          2 5 5 8 9
          2 3 3 6 0
            2 2 2 9 9
            2 0 4 4 0
              1 8 5 9 2
              1 7 5 2 0
                1 0 7 2
```

Solution for page 51 (bottom).

```
                8 9 4 7
1 5 6 | 1 3 9 5 7 9 8
        1 2 4 8
          1 4 7 7
          1 4 0 4
            7 3 9
            6 2 4
            1 1 5 8
            1 0 9 2
                6 6
```

Solution for page 91 (bottom).

75	60	91	18	34	85	50	101	27	44
108	12	36	79	53	97	22	46	69	63
29	81	68	94	25	40	71	58	104	15
62	96	19	43	77	52	106	9	33	88
21	47	74	55	100	11	38	84	65	90
76	49	103	17	32	86	59	93	28	42
107	14	35	80	61	98	24	45	70	51
30	83	67	92	26	39	73	57	102	16
54	95	20	41	78	64	105	10	31	87
23	48	72	66	99	13	37	82	56	89

Solution for page 36 (top).

The secret word is: QUAKE

Solution for page 75 (top).

(1) God save you from a bad neighbor and from a beginner on the fiddle.

(2) Argue for your limitations and, sure enough, they're yours.

(3) Never give advice in a crowd.

(4) Make the most of yourself, for that is all there is of you.

(5) Silent gratitude isn't very much use to anyone.

Solution for page 44 (bottom).

```
                  6 2 6 4
1 3 6 3 | 8 5 3 9 1 2 5
          8 1 7 8
            3 6 1 1
            2 7 2 6
                8 8 5 2
                8 1 7 8
                  6 7 4 5
                  5 4 5 2
                    1 2 9 3
```

Solution for page 92 (bottom).

126	168	30	72	114
162	54	66	108	120
48	60	102	144	156
84	96	138	150	42
90	132	174	36	78

Solution for page 52 (top).

```
                  4 7 3 8
1 3 0 0 | 6 1 5 9 9 4 7
          5 2 0 0
            9 5 9 9
            9 1 0 0
              4 9 9 4
              3 9 0 0
              1 0 9 4 7
              1 0 4 0 0
                    5 4 7
```

118

Solution for page 67 (bottom).

(1) Franklin Pierce & William R. King

(2) Richard M. Nixon & Gerald R. Ford

(3) Ulysses S. Grant & Henry Wilson

(4) James Madison & Daniel T. Tompkins

(5) Richard M. Nixon & Spiro T. Agnew

Solution for page 30 (bottom).

2	6	9	7	4	8	3	5	1
8	5	1	3	9	6	7	4	2
4	7	3	5	1	2	9	8	6
9	8	7	1	6	3	4	2	5
1	2	4	9	7	5	8	6	3
6	3	5	2	8	4	1	9	7
7	1	6	8	2	9	5	3	4
3	9	2	4	5	7	6	1	8
5	4	8	6	3	1	2	7	9

Solution for page 21.

```
              A
        B  :  A
              B
    D             C
              C
        D  :  C
              D
  E                   H
              E
        E  :  F
              F
  E                   H
              G
        G  :  H
              H
J                         I
              I
        J  :  I
              J
    J             I
              K
        K  :  L
              L
J                     I
              M
        N  :  M
              N
    P             M
              O
        P  :  O
              P
```

Solution for page 88 (bottom).

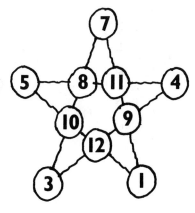

119

Solution for page 68 (bottom).

(1) He who cannot dance blames the floor.

(2) Faults are thick where love is thin.

(3) Adventure is just a romantic word for trouble.

(4) There is no such thing as darkness, only a failure to see.

(5) Treat your guest as a guest for two days; then give him a hoe.

Solution for page 22.

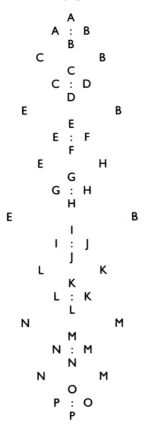

```
              A
          A : B
              B
      C           B
              C
          C : D
              D
    E                 B
              E
          E : F
              F
      E           H
              G
          G : H
              H
  E                   B
              I
          I : J
              J
      L           K
              K
          L : K
              L
    N                 M
              M
          N : M
              N
      N           M
              O
          P : O
              P
```

Solution for page 31 (top).

1	7	3	8	4	2	9	5	6
2	5	6	9	3	7	8	4	1
4	8	9	5	6	1	3	2	7
3	2	8	6	7	9	4	1	5
6	1	4	3	8	5	2	7	9
7	9	5	1	2	4	6	3	8
8	6	7	2	1	3	5	9	4
9	3	1	4	5	8	7	6	2
5	4	2	7	9	6	1	8	3

Solution for page 90 (top).

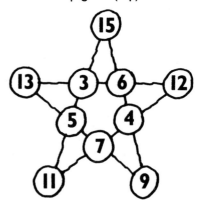

Solution for page 36 (middle).

The secret word is: RENTS

Solution for page 76 (bottom).

(1) You can have anything you want but not everything you want.

(2) Solitude is a good place to visit but a poor place to stay.

(3) Minds are like parachutes; they only function when open.

(4) That which is brief, if it be good, is good twice over.

(5) Hindsight is an exact science.

Solution for page 45 (top).

```
              7 3 5 3
7 4 2 | 5 4 5 6 4 6 7
        5 1 9 4
        -------
          2 6 2 4
          2 2 2 6
          -------
            3 9 8 6
            3 7 1 0
            -------
              2 7 6 7
              2 2 2 6
              -------
                5 4 1
```

Solution for page 52 (bottom).

```
              8 2 6 4
9 0 4 | 7 4 7 0 8 0 1
        7 2 3 2
        -------
          2 3 8 8
          1 8 0 8
          -------
            5 8 0 0
            5 4 2 4
            -------
              3 7 6 1
              3 6 1 6
              -------
                1 4 5
```

Solution for page 83 (bottom).

153	27	36	126
54	108	99	81
90	72	63	117
45	135	144	18

Solution for page 37 (middle).

The secret word is: SWAMI

Solution for page 77 (top).

(1) Feelings are everywhere. Be gentle.

(2) He who has a choice has trouble.

(3) Truth has no special time of its own. Its hour is now—always.

(4) Enough is abundance to the wise.

(5) You can put up a wall or build a bridge; the choice is yours.

Solution for page 45 (bottom).

```
                  1 0 8 9
         ┌─────────────────
1 3 6 0 │ 1 4 8 1 3 7 1
          1 3 6 0
          ─────────
            1 2 1 3 7
            1 0 8 8 0
            ─────────
              1 2 5 7 1
              1 2 2 4 0
              ─────────
                  3 3 1
```

Solution for page 53 (top).

```
                5 3 3 0
       ┌─────────────────
4 8 1 │ 2 5 6 4 0 3 2
        2 4 0 5
        ─────────
          1 5 9 0
          1 4 4 3
          ─────────
            1 4 7 3
            1 4 4 3
            ─────────
                3 0 2
```

Solution for page 89 (top).

96	12	18	78
30	66	60	48
54	42	36	72
24	84	90	6

Solution for page 67 (top).

(1) The only way to have a friend is to be one.

(2) Make the most of yourself, for that is all there is of you.

(3) Whoever wants to reach a distant goal must take many small steps.

(4) A perch in the pot is better than a salmon in the sea.

(5) Truth has no special time of its own. Its hour is now— always.

Solution for page 31 (bottom).

6	9	3	2	7	8	5	4	1
8	4	1	5	3	9	2	7	6
7	2	5	4	1	6	3	8	9
3	8	2	1	9	5	7	6	4
1	6	7	3	2	4	8	9	5
9	5	4	6	8	7	1	3	2
2	1	9	8	6	3	4	5	7
5	3	6	7	4	2	9	1	8
4	7	8	9	5	1	6	2	3

Solution for page 23.

```
              A
          A : B
              B
      D           B
              C
          D : C
              D
  D                   H
              E
          E : F
              F
      G           H
              G
          G : H
              H
  J                   H
              I
          J : I
              J
      J           L
              K
          K : L
              L
  J                   L
              M
          N : M
              N
      O           P
              O
          O : P
              P
```

Solution for page 90 (middle).

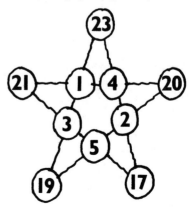

123

Solution for page 69 (top).

(1) To teach is to learn twice.

(2) No one needs a recipe for leftover lobster.

(3) I prefer the dreams of the future to the history of the past.

(4) Argue for your limitations and, sure enough, they're yours.

(5) Don't bunt. Aim out of the ball park.

Solution for page 58 (bottom).

(1) Nothing makes us better listeners than hearing our name mentioned.

(2) A rut is a grave with the ends kicked out.

(3) Success is not a journey, but a destination.

(4) There is no success without risk.

(5) Life is what happens to us while we're making plans for life.

Solution for page 77 (bottom).

(1) The silver lining is easier to find in someone else's cloud.

(2) The ship in the harbor is safe, but that's not what it was made for.

(3) I prefer the dreams of the future to the history of the past.

(4) Getting even throws everything out of balance.

(5) Any fool can criticize, condemn and complain—and most do.

Solution for page 46 (top).

```
            5 0 7 9
       _____
4 7 3 | 2 4 0 2 7 1 2
        2 3 6 5
        _____
          3 7 7 1
          3 3 1 1
          _____
            4 6 0 2
            4 2 5 7
            _____
              3 4 5
```

Solution for page 91 (top).

91	42	77
56	70	84
63	98	49

Solution for page 37 (middle).

The secret word is: USAGE

Solution for page 70 (bottom).

(1) Minds are like parachutes; they only function when open.

(2) Practice does not make perfect; perfect practice makes perfect.

(3) Why not go out on a limb? That's where the fruit is.

(4) Anyone who's always raising the roof rarely has much in the attic.

(5) Nothing ages people like not thinking.

Solution for page 64 (bottom).

(1) The only things we keep are the things we give away.

(2) Only the wearer knows where the shoe pinches.

(3) A monkey in silk is still a monkey.

(4) There's a great difference between knowing a thing & understanding it.

(5) Fears are educated into us and can, if we wish, be educated out.

Solution for page 53 (bottom).

```
                    7 1 9 3
    3 6 7 | 2 6 4 0 0 0 5
            2 5 6 9
                7 1 0
                3 6 7
                3 4 3 0
                3 3 0 3
                    1 2 7 5
                    1 1 0 1
                        1 7 4
```

Solution for page 90 (bottom).

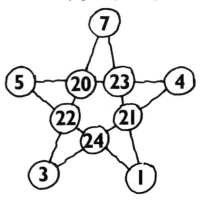

125

Solution for page 75 (bottom).

(1) The best way to destroy an enemy is to make him your friend.

(2) Against every great & noble endeavor stand a million mediocre minds.

(3) You don't drown by falling into the water, but by staying in it.

(4) Treat your guest as a guest for two days; then give him a hoe.

(5) The only way to have a friend is to be one.

Solution for page 59 (top).

(1) You don't drown by falling into the water, but by staying in it.

(2) Few things are created and perfected at the same moment.

(3) Your life is not a dress rehearsal.

(4) Success comes in cans; failure in can'ts.

(5) He who indulges, . . . bulges.

Solution for page 78 (top).

(1) The most solid stone in a structure is the lowest in the foundation.

(2) The trick is growing up without growing old.

(3) The person who doesn't read has little advantage over one who can't.

(4) When you need salt, sugar won't do.

(5) An egotist is a person who is never in doubt but often in error.

Solution for page 46 (bottom).

```
                        1 8 3 4
        1 0 2 2 | 1 8 7 5 0 9 0
                  1 0 2 2
                  -------
                    8 5 3 0
                    8 1 7 6
                    -------
                      3 5 4 9
                      3 0 6 6
                      -------
                        4 8 3 0
                        4 0 8 8
                        -------
                            7 4 2
```

Solution for page 85 (bottom).

135	72	117
90	108	126
99	144	81

INDEX